JAP AN

Travel with Marco Polo Insider Tips

INSIDER TIP
Your shortcut to a great experience

MARCO POLO
TOP HIGHLIGHTS

SHIRETOKO NATIONAL PARK ⭐

Hiking and boat tours in spectacular natural surroundings: watch bears catching salmon for breakfast!

📷 *Tip: Take a high-quality zoom lens and a camera that will withstand splashing water.*

➤ p. 46, The North

MORI BUILDING DIGITAL ART MUSEUM: TEAMLAB BORDERLESS ⭐

Digital, interactive art with light animations that will make your creative juices flow. Let your imagination guide you through this labyrinth!

📷 *Tip: The more you get involved, the cooler your photos will be. Touch what you see: elephants turn into flowers, and graphic characters trigger rain and lightning.*

➤ p. 66, Tokyo & the East

TOSHOGU SHRINE ⭐

The magnificent complex in Nikko, with its many temples and shrines, is surrounded by majestic cedar woods.

📷 *Tip: In the afternoon the trees render the scenery somewhat dark, so it's better to take photographs in the morning.*

➤ p. 72, Tokyo & the East

KAMAKURA ⭐

The old imperial city has a wealth of cultural artefacts – the biggest being the Great Buddha Daibutsu sitting on a lotus flower.

➤ p. 74, Tokyo & the East

KAIYUKAN AQUARIUM ⭐

Get up close to whale sharks, rays and jellyfish without getting wet – enjoy the fascinating underwater worlds in Osaka.

➤ p. 96, Central Japan

MIYAJIMA ⭐
Close to Hiroshima, the bright red gate of the Itsukushima Shrine is visible for miles offshore.
📷 *Tip: If you wait for high tide, the gate and the shrine behind it look as if they are floating on the water.*

➤ p. 109, The West

WHALE WATCHING OFF OKINAWA ⭐
A large number of these giants of the ocean congregate around Za-mami-jima Island: an unforgettable experience!

➤ p. 134, The South

NAOSHIMA ⭐
Be inspired by modern art and museum buildings designed by famous architects on this island in the Seto Inland Sea.
📷 *Tip: Yayoi Kusama's giant pumpkin installation on the shore makes a good picture.*

➤ p. 137, Discovery Tours

JIGOKUDANI SNOW MONKEY PARK ⭐
Japanese macaques love bathing in hot springs in winter as much as people – watch them in this valley in the Nagano Mountains.

➤ p. 83, Central Japan

FUSHIMI INARI-TAISHA ⭐
Countless orange gates line the path uphill – a unique sight at Japan's biggest fox shrine in Kyoto (photo).

➤ p. 90, Central Japan

CONTENTS

THE NORTH

CENTRAL JAPAN   TOKYO & THE EAST

THE WEST

THE SOUTH

CONTENTS

⊙   Plan your visit   ¶ Eating & drinking   🌂 Rainy day activities

¥–¥¥¥ Price categories   👜 Shopping   🦇 Budget activities

(*) Call charges apply   ▼ Nightlife   😎 Family activities

                             ⚲ Top beaches   ⚑ Classic experiences

(𝄤 A2) Pull-out map
(𝄤 a2) Tokyo street map on the pull-out map
(0) Off the pull-out map

BEST OF JAPAN

Snow-capped Mount Fuji is at its most beautiful during cherry blossom season

BEST ☂ WHEN IT RAINS

ACTIVITIES TO BRIGHTEN YOUR DAY

BE AN OLYMPIAN
You are more likely to experience snow than rain in Sapporo, but don't worry: in the *Sapporo Olympic Museum* you can ski jump in a simulator without getting soggy or run a virtual bobsleigh at 130kmh.
➤ p. 44, The North

ONE THOUSAND AND ONE STATUES
In the *Sanjusangen-do* temple in Kyoto, 1,001 life-size statues of Bodhisattva Kannon, the Goddess of Mercy, greet you. They are all slightly different – try to spot the individual features.
➤ p. 90, Central Japan

UNDERSTAND WORLD HISTORY
What does it mean when a nuclear weapon is dropped on a city? The *Hiroshima Peace Memorial Museum* and the *Nagasaki Atomic Bomb Museum* use testimonies, photographs and molten remains to tell the harrowing stories of the victims, many of whom continued to suffer for decades after the end of World War II.
➤ p. 108, The West, p. 126, The South

UNDERGROUND EXPLORATION
Explore the *Akiyoshido limestone cave*, the biggest and longest in Japan, on a well-lit trail and listen to the rushing stream and waterfalls.
➤ p. 115, The West

UNDERWATER WORLD
The *Okinawa Churaumi Aquarium* has a sensational display of species. You can touch the sea snails in the Okinawa tank, watch whale sharks at close range and admire the elegant Manta rays (photo).
➤ p. 134, The South

BEST 🐷
ON A BUDGET

FOR SMALLER WALLETS

EAT FOR LESS
In the evening, many department stores and supermarkets reduce their prices for freshly prepared food by up to 50 per cent. Get a bento box and enjoy a picnic outdoors.

SHOP FOR 100 YEN
Family and friends may ask you to get them all kinds of things from Japan. Good value for money is to be found in the *100-yen shops*. For approximately 60 pence per item, you can get anything from chopsticks and bowls to snacks – and objects you may never have considered before, such as a container to keep your banana in.

DISCOUNT CINEMA TICKETS
Going to the cinema can be expensive in Japan. It's cheaper to get discounted tickets from specialised shops or, if eligible, to go on "Ladies' Day", which is usually Wednesday. On the first day of the month, men also get a discount.

ENJOY THE BLOSSOM FOR FREE
Whether you come for people watching or for the cherry blossom (photo) – the extensive *Ueno Park* with its museums, cafés and temples is a wonderful place to visit. In summer, the lotus flower pond is particularly beautiful.
➤ p. 63, Tokyo & the East

A GLANCE UNDER THE BONNET
Factory tours at *Toyota* and *Mazda* show you how cars are manufactured on the production line. The tours are free of charge, and you can even sit in the cars; online booking is required.
➤ p. 88, Central Japan, p. 108, Western Japan

BEST WITH CHILDREN

FUN FOR YOUNG & OLD

LIMITLESS CREATIVITY

Dive into a digital sea of light and colour! In the *Mori Building Digital Art Museum: Teamlab Borderless* you can become an artist yourself. Special scanners allow both the young and the old to digitalise what they have painted and bring it to life.
➤ p. 66, Tokyo & the East

GETTING CLOSE TO DINOSAURS

Do your children love dinosaurs? Then the *Fukui Prefectural Dinosaur Museum* with its 42 complete skeletons will be a hit. You can hunt for fossils in the museum's quarry.
➤ p. 86, Central Japan

WHITEWATER FUN

Pure adrenaline, but don't worry: the skippers who safely steer the boats close to the rocks and through the rapids of the *Hozugawa River* north-west of Kyoto know what they are doing.
➤ p. 92, Central Japan

FUN IN THE THEME PARK

Visit *Universal Studios Japan* in Osaka and travel through movie worlds from *Jurassic Park* to *Harry Potter*. Are you brave enough for the rollercoaster ride?
➤ p. 97, Central Japan

WHALE WATCHING

From late December to early April, the islands of *Okinawa* attract many whales – a great opportunity to see these giants of the ocean. If this is not when or where you are travelling, the north of Japan also offers whale watching in the *Shiretoko National Park* between May and October, when you may encounter sperm whales, orcas, dolphins and seals.
➤ p. 134, The South, p. 47, The North

BEST 🚩

CLASSIC EXPERIENCES

ONLY IN JAPAN

ARTWORKS ON WHEELS
Artisans prepare for many weeks to get the floats ready for the *Nebuta Matsuri* festival in Aomori. The floats are several metres tall, lit from the inside and made of wood, wire and painted paper. They are carried through the city centre, accompanied by drummers and dancers.
➤ p. 49, The North

SWIM WITH DOLPHINS
You won't get any closer to wild dolphins than this. On the Izu island of *Mikurajima*, which belongs to Tokyo, you can swim with them in summer.
➤ p. 77, Tokyo & the East

RURAL IDYLL
High in the mountains is *Shirakawa-go*, a group of small villages with unique farmhouses whose steep roofs resemble hands that are folded for prayer. An idyllic location (photo).
➤ p. 87, Central Japan

HOLY VILLAGE
Koya-san is a remote village in the mountains of Wakayama. It is a centre of Shingon Buddhism with 100 temples, pagodas, atmospheric cemeteries and stone gardens. Staying overnight in a temple that serves vegetarian monk cuisine is an extraordinary experience.
➤ p. 98, Central Japan

PEACE & POWER
Its ponds and streams, bamboo groves and pine trees make the *Sengan-en Garden* a marvellous sight – especially with the silhouette of the active volcano of Sakurajima in the background. Different varieties of cherry allow you to see the blossom spectacle here from the end of January to mid-April.
➤ p. 130, The South

GET TO KNOW JAPAN

Japan's *Shinkansen* is reliable, safe and punctual

DISCOVER JAPAN

Central Tokyo

At a shrine in the Tokyo business district of Toranomon, the faithful pull at colourful ribbons. A bell rings. The visitors, among them businesspeople in dark suits, throw coins into a wooden box. They clap and bow and clap again. Trees and wooden cabins stood here in centuries gone by, but today the sanctuary is surrounded by countless office blocks of glass and steel. The new and the old side by side and interwoven – this is typical for Tokyo and for the country as a whole.

COUNTLESS ISLANDS

"What am I – and how many?" If Japan was asking this question about itself, the answer might be: four large islands and thousands of small ones. This island nation in East Asia comprises the four main islands of Hokkaido, Honshu,

660-585 BCE
Reign of Japan's first mythical emperor, Jimmu

794-1192
Heian period: Kyoto is the capital

1192-1333
Kamakura is the capital

1603-1868
Edo period: unification of the empire, isolationist policy towards the outside world, a cultural Golden Age

1868
Meiji restoration: strengthening of imperial power

1895-1945
Wars with China and Russia; Taiwan and Korea become colonies

Shikoku and Kyushu as well as almost 7,000 other islands, of which a mere 430 are inhabited. But even if you stayed just on the biggest island, Honshu, you may be forgiven for thinking that you were crossing several countries and climatic zones. While the side of the country that faces the Sea of Japan gets a lot of snow and has a climate that resembles northern Europe, its Pacific side has summers that are humid and damp – especially in the concrete jungles of Tokyo and Osaka – while the winters are sunny and pleasantly mild, with temperatures hardly ever dropping below zero. Very different again are the island chains of Amami and Okinawa where Japan displays its subtropical side, which few foreigners know about, with an average temperature of 23.5°C, white sandy beaches and turquoise sea.

MOUNTAINS, EARTHQUAKES & GODS

When you're in Tokyo's urban jungle, it's hard to conceive of the fact that 80 per cent of Japan's landmass consists of mountains, including dormant – and a few active – volcanoes. The best known is also the highest: Mount Fuji, at 3,776m, is a symbol of Japan and venerated as a holy mountain by the country's nature religion of Shintoism. Mount Fuji last erupted in 1707. In 1923, Tokyo was destroyed by a massive earthquake and subsequent fire – and Kobe suffered the same fate in 1995. In the past century, the Pacific coast witnessed several tsunamis that were triggered by seaquakes. In Japan, children learn early in life how to manage nature's hazards. However, the entire population, as well as some

1941
Attack on Pearl Harbour

1945
Atomic bombs dropped on Hiroshima and Nagasaki

Around 1990
The 1980s megaboom is followed by economic decline

1989–2019
Heisei period under Emperor Akihito is characterised by peace and economic stagnation

2011
Tsunami and nuclear catastrophe in Fukushima

2019
Coronation of Emperor Naruhito introduces the new "Reiwa" period

monkeys, are passionate about enjoying the positive aspects of the country's tricky geology – its many hot springs.

SKYSCRAPERS & WOODEN HOUSES

People are under the impression that Japanese houses are tiny, but that's not true. If you visit the countryside, you will find enormous wooden farmhouses with heavy tiled roofs and enough space for several generations of the same family. However, the typical living space in Tokyo is much smaller. "Tokyo is so busy and crowded," say people in Japan's countryside who live in small settlements and close-knit communities of farmers or fishermen – growing rice requires teamwork, after all. People in the rural areas often eat what they grow in their own gardens, while townspeople tend to eat out or get ready meals from convenience stores that are open around the clock.

LONELY HEARTS

In Japan, you will see "salarymen" and an increasing number of "salarywomen" everywhere. Dark suits with a shirt and tie are mandatory for men – except in the summer during the "cool biz" time – while the dress code for women specifies a suit and high heels. Coming to the office without professionally manicured nails or makeup is regarded as a faux pas. However, working extremely long hours into the night plus commutes of an hour or longer can't be helpful to the dating game; Japan's singletons often struggle to find life partners. Marriage is on the decrease, and the average marriage age has risen to above 30, similar to Europe.

YOUNG WORKERS WANTED

Politicians are keen to rejuvenate Japan, which has become a "super-aging society". There are incentives for families, both financial and in terms of childcare support. At the same time, businesses are encouraged to incentivise women to keep them in the workforce; this is because immigration is an uneasy subject for a country that regards itself as homogenous. Since World War II, Japanese politics has been dominated by the conservative Liberal Democrats who, in recent years, have increasingly turned to the right under Prime Minister Shinzo Abe. And what about the geishas, ninjas and samurais, cosplay, maid cafés and Pokémon? These are all part of Japan's rich culture too. Enjoy new discoveries and surprises every day – but start saving now because once you get hooked on all things Japanese, it's a hard habit to break.

AT A GLANCE

126,200,000
inhabitants, of which 38 million live in the metropolitan region of Tokyo
UK: 67 million

5,520,000
vending machines in the country

UK: approx. 1.2 million

29,000km
of coastline
UK: 12,400km

378,000km^2
area

UK: 242,500km^2

HIGHEST PEAK: MOUNT FUJI
3,776m
Ben Nevis: 1,345m

AVERAGE BIRTH RATE

1.43
children per woman

UK: 1.59

ALPHABET
2,136
characters to be learned by Japanese school children

⭐ MOST EXPENSIVE TUNA

£2.2 million was paid for a 278kg tuna at the New Year's auction 2019 in the Tokyo fish market.

SHINJUKU
Busiest railway station in the world with 3.5 million passengers per day

HIGHEST TELEVISION TOWER IN THE WORLD
Tokyo Skytree (634m)

Longest continuous imperial line in the world
2,700 years

UNDERSTAND JAPAN

FACE MASKS

Wearing a face mask is perfectly normal in Japan, and was even before the Coronavirus pandemic – and not only for those dealing with patients, handling foodstuffs or working in a laboratory. When a Japanese person has a cold, their fellow citizens expect them to wear a mask, and during flu season, most commuters in crowded trains wear masks to protect themselves from the virus. Japanese doctors advise people to wear masks for protection against allergens, such as tree pollen, and in winter, the mask warms your face.

FAKE FOOD

In Japan it is easy to travel and eat well without speaking the language. Many restaurants display their dishes – made of plastic – in the window. Just point to one to order it.

INSIDER TIP
Take a bite!

You can also buy these food models/samples *(shokuhin sanpuru)* as a souvenir. What about a slice of fake ham for a bookmark?

OLYMPIA

The monorail from Haneda Airport to the city centre and the Shinkansen bullet train to Osaka are from an era when Tokyo hosted the first Olympic Games to be held in Asia in 1964, during the Japanese economic miracle. The building boom made the city more practical but not necessarily prettier. Due to a lack of space, the monorail and the new city motorway were put on stilts above the canals, which was not just bad for the fishermen but also for the water quality. Behind the scenes, corruption and the Japanese mafia ruled the roost. After hosting the Winter Olympics in Sapporo in 1972 and in Nagano in 1998, Tokyo was again host in 2021. Although the construction boom was nothing like that in 1964, it was still considerable, with old houses disappearing and hotels being opened in skyscrapers. There was a controversy surrounding the National Stadium, which was originally designed by British architect Zaha Hadid, but excessive costs led to the project being cancelled. In the end, Japanese architect Kengo Kuma was commissioned.

THE IMPERIAL FAMILY

Until the end of World War II, the Emperor was seen as god-like in Japan. The people heard his voice for the first time when he announced the country's capitulation on the radio. The post-war constitution declares the *tenno* as a symbol of the state without any political function. However, both Emperor Hirohito and his successor Akihito (who abdicated in 2019) actively promoted peace and reconciliation by visiting neighbouring countries, for example, which had suffered from war and occupation. Despite the odd empress in the country's history, since 1889 the law only permits male successors in the

ドリーチキンと
オムライス

海の幸トマトソース
オムライス
767kcal (税込) **¥1,030**

和風きのこの
オムライス
584kcal (税込) **¥1,030**

南欧風ポテトサラダ
252kcal (税込)
¥610

ソーセージの
オーブン焼き
584kcal (税込) **¥610**

チキンのオーブ
545kcal (税込) **¥5**

"I'll have this one": point to the fake food to get the real dish

Imperial line. When Crown Prince (now Emperor) Naruhito and his wife, Masako, had a girl named Aiko, the Japanese authorities considered changing the law to avoid a succession crisis. However, this debate ceased when Kiko of Akishino, the wife of Naruhito's younger brother, gave birth to a boy in 2006. Women don't have it easy in other ways either: if a female member of the Imperial family marries, she loses her aristocratic status. When Sayako, the only daughter of Emperor Akihito and Empress Michiko, married a Tokyo city planner in 2005, she had to leave her family home. From that point onwards, she and her husband lived in a one-bedroom flat, and she had to learn how to shop for food and furniture.

IMPERIAL CALENDAR

Despite using the Gregorian calendar, like many other nations, Japan also has its own version, which counts the years from the Emperor's coronation. Akihito's accession in 1989 was the beginning of the Heisei period, thereby concluding the Showa period which had applied since 1926 under his father Hirohito. In 2019, Akihito's son Naruhito came to the Chrysanthemum Throne, which means that Japan entered the Reiwa period in May 2019. The new name doesn't just apply to calendars and official forms, but also to the entire world of IT, comparable to the Millennium bug.

LUCKY CHARMS

You are not simply lucky in Japan, you buy your luck – or at least try to. At temples and shrines you can shake wooden boxes, pick a stick with a number from the box and read the corresponding fortune note *(omikuji)*, which is sometimes in English. If your fortune is considered good, keep the paper note as a lucky charm. If not, tie it to a structure in the temple precinct: the gods will look after it! Otherwise last forever either. The advice is to replace your lucky charms after one year.

DISCRIMINATION AGAINST MOTHERS

One in four female Japanese employees has experienced *matahara* (maternity harassment) or discrimination during pregnancy. Pregnant women may be teased, bullied, demoted, get a reduced salary or out-

Will you be lucky in love? The fortune note will tell you!

get an *omamori*, a pretty embroidered fabric bag filled with prayers (approx. £5). Unlucky years *(yakudoshi)* in Japan are the ages of 19, 33, 37 and 61 for women and 25, 42 and 61 for men, plus an unlucky year beforehand and afterwards, watch out! If you are predetermined to be unlucky in a certain year, it is recommended that you postpone life-changing decisions or at least proceed with extra caution. On the other hand, good fortune doesn't

right dismissed. Sayaka Osakabe from Tokyo is partly responsible for introducing the term *matahara* to everyday language. In 2014, she founded Matahara Net, a charity that supports women. Her boss had tried to force her to decide between her job and her child. "If you stay at home for a week because of a cold, that's OK, but if you can't work because you are pregnant, then that's your own fault," says the women's rights activist. In 2015 she was awarded the US government's International Women of Courage Award, in person by Michelle Obama. The Global Gender Gap Report by the World Economic Forum, which measures the level of gender equality every year, regularly places Japan in the last quartile of 140 countries and far behind other industrialised nations.

WHITE LIES

In Japanese, *honne* is the word for sincere emotions, while *tatemae* is the façade that we show to the world – a kind of social behaviour that is probably more common in Japan than in other parts of the world. Do Japanese people tend to lie? Not by intention, but they often behave in way to avoid conflict and maintain harmony between people. In group-focussed Japan, *tatemae* (white lies) are designed as a way to promote politeness. This is often explained by the country's history as a *shimaguni* (land of islands). If you want to know what someone really thinks or to drop your mask for a moment or two, then a group setting with a bit of alcohol is the ideal place. If you go too far, you can blame it on the drink – an excuse which the Japanese accept for almost any misbehaviour. However, if things go wrong during your travels and you are close to blowing your top, it is best to resort to *tatemae* and to question things in a friendly but insistent manner. Showing emotion, raising your voice and losing your temper – such behaviour is seen as immature and will rarely get you anywhere.

TRUE OR FALSE?

RAW FISH & RICE EVERY DAY

The Japanese eat sushi day in, day out. Well, not quite. After all, the English don't have Yorkshire pudding every day, do they? Raw fish on vinegared rice has conquered the world, meaning that many visitors to Japan want to spend some time at a *kaitenzushi* – a restaurant where sushi is served on a conveyor belt. The Japanese, on the other hand, tend to eat sushi on special occasions. The conveyor-belt restaurants may be popular with (hungry) families on a budget, but those in the know enjoy eating at the counter where they can watch the chef's skilful fingers at work.

CRAZY ANIME & MANGA FANS

When Akihiko Kondo, an inconspicuous school employee, married the virtual singer Hatsune Miku in 2018, he made headlines around the world. While the marriage is not legally acknowledged, the wedding was like any wedding between real flesh-and-blood people and certainly as expensive. It is true that manga and anime are important phenomena in the country, but such eccentric enthusiasm for a singing hologram with turquoise twin ponytails and a miniskirt is too much for most Japanese.

PACKAGING NIGHTMARE

A roll of cellotape, which is already packaged, is then placed in a separate plastic bag, which is put in yet another bigger plastic bag that contains the other items you have bought. Sadly, this is a common scenario in Japan! Thankfully, more and more supermarkets encourage their customers to bring their own bags and are charging for plastic bags. An exception are the big exclusive department stores who are keen for their logo to be seen.

DATING

In Japan there are clearly defined lines of separation between the sexes from an early age. In order to find a date, singles go to *gokon*, informal dating parties where the event organisers try to get an even match between men and women. Much more serious are the *o-miai* (meetings) where marriage matches are made. These events were still standard for today's generation of grandparents. Nowadays, more people marry for love, but marriages of convenience continue to play a role, especially for the over-35s. This is because, if you want to have children in Japan, you need to be married. Only two per cent of babies are born out of wedlock. However, a stumbling block on the way to married bliss is cash. Japanese men need to earn about 4 million yen a year (£24,500) in order to be considered a sensible match by the women. Despite changing gender roles in society, most Japanese regard the man as the breadwinner, while the woman is responsible for bringing up the children. Japanese women also see the role of a "professional housewife" *(sengyoshufu)* as attractive. Fear of financial commitments and restrictions of their freedom are cited by an increasing number of young people as reasons for not getting married and not having children at all.

ULTRANATIONALISTS

During your stay in Tokyo, you may see big black or white trucks displaying the national flag. Their loudspeakers play martial marches, the national anthem and political slogans. The *uyoku*, right-wing ultranationalists, promote militarism, deny Japan's World War II war crimes (e.g. forced prostitution and the 1937 Nanking massacre) and intend to restore the *tenno* to power. These nationalists are also frequently seen at the Yasukuni Jinja shrine in Tokyo, where they commemorate not only the 2.5 million regular soldiers who died during the war but also 14 men who are regarded as war criminals. As a result, both China and Korea perceive the visits of high-ranking Japanese politicians to the shrine as an affront.

ROBOTIC FRIENDS

The Japanese have a playful attitude to robots and have experimented for many years with humanoid beings made of wire, plastic and steel who are intended to become much more clever in the future thanks to artificial intelligence. The hope is that robots will be able to compensate for a lack of human labour in a society that is both ageing and decreasing in numbers.

Robot dogs, robot reception staff, robot chefs – why not? Many agree with Tomomi Ota, a woman in her early thirties, who lives with a humanoid robot in Tokyo; she sees robots as a new category of existence alongside humans and pets, and keenly observes how the environment affects her artificial companion. Interestingly, despite technological progress, Japan can be wonderfully old-fashioned at times: for example, the fax machine continues to be popular in this high-tech nation.

WITHDRAWAL

At the beginning it is often bullying at school, while for others it is problems at university or the loss of their job. There are many reasons why people withdraw from life and retreat to their own home. It is estimated that there are one million people in Japan who, on average, haven't left their front door for eleven years and who mostly stay in their childhood bedroom. These people are called *hikikomori*. Those who manage to escape this trap talk of the pressure to conform in Japanese society, where someone who leaves the well-trodden path has little chance of a return. Psychological support is basically non-existent, added to which *gaman* – patience or the ability to endure tragedy – is a cherished virtue in Japan.

Who is the robot here, and is that really a fax machine in the corner?

EATING
SHOPPING
SPORT

Fresh and pickled vegetables for sale

EATING & DRINKING

Japanese cuisine is much more than just raw fish, served either as sashimi or with rice as sushi. It is incredibly varied and regarded as one of the most sophisticated cuisines in the world. In Japan, people distinguish between five tastes: salty, sweet, sour, bitter and *umami* (savoury). Both the placement of food on the plate and the choice of cutlery are given high importance.

JAPANESE PUBS

After work, Japan's workers relax in cosy *izakaya* pubs, which are often divided into separate booths with seating on tatami rice-straw mats. These pubs are lively. The staff will greet you with a loud *"irasshaimase"* (welcome) when you arrive and send on your way with a hearty *"arigato gozaimashita"* (thank you very much) at the end of your visit. The food menu is both comprehensive and diverse. Often you will

be served a chargeable snack as an hors d'oeuvre (¥300–600). You may struggle to find non-smoking areas.

SEASONAL CUISINE

In Japan you won't need a calendar. Just go to the supermarket or a restaurant and see what's on offer: *sansai* (fresh wild vegetables) are on offer in spring, and pumpkin and sweet chestnuts in autumn. The refined *kaiseki* cuisine, in particular, focuses on fresh seasonal ingredients. Instead of altering the taste with spices and sauces, the intrinsic flavours of the produce are highlighted.

REGIONAL DIFFERENCES

The Japanese love regional specialities. In the area around Tokyo, for example, noodle dishes are served in a *dashi* broth of tuna flakes and a dark soy sauce, whereas, in central Japan, dashi is made of seaweed and bonito with a

Beautifully displayed: fish and seafood (left), peaches in luxury wrapping (right)

lighter soy sauce. The Okinawa Islands produce ingredients such as *goya* (bitter cucumber) and *umibudo* (green algae) which are distinctly different from anything else in the country.

FREE WATER & TEA

When you enter a restaurant, please wait to be seated. At the table you will be served ice-cold tap water or Japanese tea (green tea or barley tea) – for free! You will also get an *oshibori*, a small wet flannel, hot in winter and cold in summer, which is only to be used to wipe your hands. The tea at the end of your meal is also on the house.

NO SPECIAL REQUIREMENTS

People in Japan have clear ideas on how dishes must be prepared and should taste. Therefore, if you have special dietary requirements – whether this is due to allergies, food intolerance or personal beliefs – it may be hard to

find variations of dishes. If you follow a gluten-free, lactose-free, vegetarian or vegan diet, you should telephone or research a suitable restaurant beforehand. Vegetarians are (mostly) well catered for with *shojin-ryori*, the vegetarian dishes for Buddhist monks.

TABLE MANNERS

The Japanese don't say "enjoy your meal"; instead they say *"itadakimasu"* ("I humbly receive") and briefly join their hands in front of their chest. Chopsticks *(o-hashi)* are the proper eating implements to use for most dishes. Please don't wave them around or impale your food with them, and under no circumstances stick them upright into the rice or pass food from chopstick to chopstick; to the Japanese such table manners are reminiscent of funeral rites. If you take food from a sharing plate, turn your chopsticks around so that you're using the broader end that hasn't been in your mouth. If you are served rice in a separate bowl, take the bowl into your hand when eating. If you empty the bowl completely, you show respect towards this staple foodstuff which is almost sacred to the people of Japan. Try to enjoy the special taste of Japanese rice rather than drowning it in soy sauce. Noodle soups are loudly slurped – because this way they are said to taste even better. After your meal, you say *"go-chiso-sama deshita"* ("this was delicious") – both if you are someone's guest or in a restaurant.

LIQUID RICE & WHISKY

The Japanese love rice in all its forms, including fermented as rice wine, known as *sake* – a word for alcohol in general – or *nihonshu*. The latter is brewed from rice, water, koji mould and yeast and is usually drunk chilled, but sometimes warm in winter. The quality of *nihonshu* is determined by how much the rice has been "polished" or refined: *ginjo* contains rice that has been polished to no more than 60 per cent of its original size; *daiginjo* is refined to 50 per cent. Rice wine has 13 to 18 per cent alcohol. A stronger drink is *shochu*, which is made of sweet potatoes, barley, rice, buckwheat or sugarcane with 25 to 37 per cent alcohol. It is often drunk diluted with (hot) water. Also popular is *umeshu*, a sweet and fruity liqueur from the ume apricot, often drunk on ice or diluted with soda. By the way, don't pour yourself a drink without serving other people first. If you are

INSIDER TIP
Look after others!

being poured a drink by someone else, hold your glass towards the other person with both hands.

Whisky has been produced commercially in Japan for the past 100 years – in Scottish fashion, but with a Japanese twist: the whisky is stored in barrels of local wood or in barrels that previously contained *umeshu* liqueur. Since Bill Murray made an advertisement for Suntory in the movie *Lost in Translation*, Japanese whisky has become internationally known and won several awards. In Japan, whisky is mostly drunk diluted with water or soda.

FOOD FROM THE BOX

Bento is the term for Japanese lunch boxes which are mostly filled with fish, meat, pickled and cooked vegetables and rice. Delicious versions are sold in the basements of department stores *(depachika)*, but they are cheaper in supermarkets and convenience stores. For travelling on the Shinkansen, *ekiben* bentos are practical and available at railway stations (but please don't eat on the tube!). Handy snacks include *onigiri* rice balls that are filled with sour plums or salmon, etc.

DESSERTS TO GET USED TO

Beans in sweets? Although it sounds strange, this combination is rather tasty. Sweetened floury azuki beans are a staple in many Japanese sweets, such as *shiruko*, a kind of bean soup, served with *mochi* (rice caies) and *kuri* (sweet chestnuts). *Wagashi*, Japanese confectionery, often comprises mashed bean with sugar and rice flour. In summer, jelly-like dishes are popular.

Today's Specials

Street Food

SOBA/RAMEN/UDON
A soup with buckwheat noodles (*soba*), thin wheat noodles (*ramen*) or thick wheat noodles (*udon*) and topped with vegetables, meat and fish

TAKOYAKI
Fried dough balls, filled with octopus

Vegetarian

VEGETABLE TEMPURA
Fried vegetables in dough, with salt or a light dipping sauce

DENGAKU-DOFU
Tofu, grilled and brushed with a miso paste

NABE
Vegetables and tofu, briefly cooked in stock and dipped in a sesame or *ponzu* (citrus-and-soy) sauce

Meat Dishes

SHABUSHABU
Hotpot of thinly sliced meat and vegetables, boiled in seaweed stock

OKONOMIYAKI
Hearty, thick pancakes, filled according to preference – e.g. with pork, shrimps, cheese and spring onions – and fried on a hot plate

YAKITORI
Grilled chicken skewers with salt or soy sauce

Fish & Seafood

KATSUO NO TATAKI
Bonito tuna, crisply fried on the outside, but raw on the inside, served with spring onions, ginger and garlic and seasoned with soy sauce, vinegar and lemon

HOTATE NO BATAYAKI
Scallops fried in butter

Desserts

KUZUKIRI
Glass noodles from the bean-like *kuzu* root, served with brown sugar syrup

SHOPPING

Japan can be a threat to your wallet, especially if you're a fan of Japanese arts and crafts. The attention to detail is unrivalled, as is the quality. Prices don't have a ceiling, but flea markets offer real treasures for little money, and 100-yen shops have all kinds of bargains.

BEAUTIFULLY SHARP

Tokyo's "kitchen hotspot" of Kappabashi, its fish markets or exclusive department stores offer a great selection of premium Japanese knives, with good specimens starting from around £70. Their shape depends on their intended purpose in the kitchen. Many have marbled patterns on the blade and the master craftsman's name engraved in graphic characters. Make sure that you look after your Japanese knife well and always dry it immediately.

BLOT INSTEAD OF POWDER

The humid Japanese summer makes it difficult to apply face powder because it blocks the pores while leaving your face shiny. It is **INSIDER TIP** **Lovely skin!** better to use *aburatorigami*, facial oil blotting paper, which is traditionally used by geishas. Made of the finest paper, it fits into the smallest handbag. All the big cosmetics brands like Shiseido sell them and the best-known brand is *Yojiya (yojiya.co.jp)*.

SKILFULLY WRAPPED

Many visitors to Japan are looking to buy a kimono or its summer version, the *yukata*, which is more comfortable in the heat. Both are to be found in Tokyo's luxury department stores, with more affordable versions available at the kimono chain *Tansuya* or at the *Sakaeya (kimono-sakaeya.com/Tokyo)* family business in Harajuku (Tokyo).

Colourful souvenirs: cast-iron teapots (left) and wooden sandals (right)

Here, you can also hire kimonos, get help with dressing and dress up for a small tea ceremony. Great-value kimonos and *yukatas* can be found in flea markets or second-hand shops.

ZEN OFF THE SHELF

"Less is more". The Japanese brands Muji and Uniqlo work according to this motto, offering modern Zen minimalism to take away. While Uniqlo specialises in fashion basics, from underwear to puffer jackets, Muji focuses on homewares in timeless muted colours.

POLISHED VESSELS

Making lacquerware is a craft that is thousands of years old. It is a labour-intensive craft involving numerous processes, first to produce lacquer from the lacquer tree and then to apply it to a carrier material, usually wood but also glass, leather or paper.

The resulting product is antibacterial, lightweight, durable – and absolutely beautiful! Many lacquered items are also decorated with gold and silver powder. The best-known manufacturing locations are Wajima, Yamanaka and Aizu-Wakamatsu.

FOLDED & KNOTTED

One of the most versatile souvenirs is a *tenugui*, a folded towel. It is really a hand towel, but people use it in summer to wipe up sweat or as a neckerchief. Printed with traditional patterns and motifs, it also makes a pretty and decorative item to hang on a wall. The bigger version, *furoshiki*, can be knotted into a carrier bag to carry a bento lunch box, for example, or as eco-friendly gift wrap.

SPORT & ACTIVITIES

Approximately 70 per cent of Japan's landmass is mountainous and great for hiking or skiing. The south of the country, with its numerous island chains, is ideal for watersports.

CYCLING

You may be surprised how rural and "empty" Japan can be outside the mega-cities. Many cycling routes follow the coast, for example around the Noto Peninsula (Ishikawa) or along the north coast of Hokkaido. The southern part of Shikoku also lends itself to cycling. Popular and practical, the *Shimanami Kaido (go-shimanami.jp/global/english)*, a 70-km-long, well-signposted route crosses six islands between Onomichi on Honshu and Imabari on Shikoku; you can hire bicycles, e.g. from *Giant (bicyclerental.jp/en)*, and have your luggage transported by *Sagawa (sagawa-exp.co.jp/stc/english)*.

HIKING

Traditionally, hiking had strong religious connotations in Japan – and today the tradition of venerating mountains as divine continues in the form of festivals. Even from the megalopolis of Tokyo, it is easy to go on countless day tours, ranging from easy trips to challenging expeditions. Popular and easy to climb are the mountains Takao and Mitake near Tokyo. However, for tours to the Northern Alps you should be a fit and experienced hiker. There are also multi-day trekking tours through national parks. You can combine culture and hiking at the fascinating Mount Nokogiriyama close to Tokyo (Chiba). The bizarrely shaped peak has a temple complex and a gigantic stone statue of the Buddha. If you don't like walking on

INSIDER TIP
Where the Buddha greets you

Kayaking around Okinawa: great fun, even for beginners

your own, why not join an outdoor organisation such as *Friends of the Earth (hikes from Tokyo every Sun | fee 1,000 yen | foejapan.org/en/event/hike.html)?*

KAYAKING & SUP

From northern to southern Japan, you will find countless kayaking opportunities on rivers, lakes and along the coast. Beautiful tours lead through the mangroves of Amami-Oshima (Kagoshima) and Iriomote (Okinawa). The subtropical island of Iriomote is home to a huge variety of fauna and flora, allowing you to paddle past waterfalls and jungle trails. Coastal areas, such as the turquoise waters around the Kerama Islands (Okinawa) or south-west of the Izu Peninsula not far from Tokyo, are ideal for paddling, even for beginners. More adventurous is a paddling tour through the famous red *torii gate* at Miyajima

(Hiroshima). You can even explore Tokyo on its rivers and canals *(tokyokayaking.jp)*.

INSIDER TIP
See Tokyo from the water

Kayaking outfitters often provide stand-up paddleboarding (SUP) equipment as well.

PARAGLIDING

If you want to get a bird's-eye view of Japan, take the train from Tokyo (one hour) to Joso (Ibaraki), where the *Gain Paraglider School (gain-para.com)* gets you airborne. You can do the same in Uenohara (Yamanashi) near Mount Fuji *(nishitokyo-para.jp)*. If you feel as though you have seen enough temples in Kyoto, enjoy the countryside from the air in the city of Nantan *(birds-para.com)*. On a paragliding flight in Amami-Oshima, there will only be the turquoise sea beneath you. Most operators offer courses for beginners as well as tandem flights.

RAFTING

Are you keen to skim downriver in a dinghy and master wild rapids? Then the Tonegawa River is the place to be, where Rafting World Cup qualifiers have been held. Or drive to the 200-km-long Yoshinogawa River (Kochi) on the island of Shikoku. It winds through ancient river valleys while gaining awesome speed. A quieter experience awaits you on the Himekawa River, with a view of the mountains of Hakuba. This river is also suitable for families with children.

SHOWER CLIMBING

If you feel the need to cool down in the humid Japanese summer, try *sawanobori* or Shower Climbing, where you hike uphill though cooling mountain streams. More challenging routes require a helmet and climbing gear. Peak season is between July and September. Look out for tour offers (book via local tourist information centres) north-west of Tokyo, e.g. in Gunma, Nagano and Gifu, but also in western Japan, for example in Tottori. English-speaking operators are based near Tokyo, e.g. *Canyons (canyons.jp/en)*.

SKIING & SNOWBOARDING

Japan gets a lot of snow: 20m and more in a season make the country a reliable destination for skiers. It only takes 75 minutes to travel from Tokyo to the slopes of Yuzawa (Niigata), which has several interconnected ski regions for beginners and advanced skiers alike. The Winter Olympics 1998 have made the ski resorts of Nagano famous throughout the world, such as the popular resort of Hakuba and the Shiga Kogen highlands; this is one of the biggest ski regions in Japan with slopes suitable for all levels. Apart from great slopes, Nozawa Onsen (Nagano) also has beautiful hot springs. The best powder snow in the country can be enjoyed near Hokkaido (travel by plane). English is spoken in the popular resort of Niseko, which also offers great après-ski choices. Furano is known for long slopes and Tomamu for off-piste skiing. Most ski resorts offer snowshoe hiking, but cross-country skiing is rare.

SNORKELLING & SCUBA DIVING

Japan's best spots for snorkelling and scuba diving are south of Kyushu (Yakushima, Amami-Oshima, Tanegashima) and in Okinawa. There, the air temperatures are mostly above 25°C, with pleasant water temperatures due to the Kuroshio Current. Peak season for diving is from July to mid-September with an off-season from December to March. Even beginners will love an excursion to the Kerama Islands (Okinawa), which have deep blue water, coral reefs and one of the most varied underwater worlds in the country, home to a huge number of marine animals from shellfish to boxfishes. But Okinawa also has different scenery: around Miyakojima you can dive and snorkel in limestone caves and tunnels as well as between rock formations. Ishigaki (Okinawa) is famous for the so-called "Manta Scramble" where enormous rays gather to feed on plankton.

If you want to get close to small marine life, you don't even have to leave the Tokyo area: Kozushima, one of the Izu Islands, is ideal for macro-diving for snails, crab and starfish. Ice-divers like to float through the kelp forests around the Shiretoko Peninsula on Hokkaido.

SURFING

Obviously, Japan is not as well known for surfing as Australia, but on the other hand there are virtually no reported shark attacks in Japan! The heavily defended coastline means that waves are often tamed, but there are sufficient beach breaks and river-mouth breaks. Japan's surf scene is active all year round at water temperatures between 17 and 23°C. Your best chance of a high swell is during the typhoon season from August to October. Near Tokyo you will always find surfers on the beaches of Shonan in the Kanagawa Prefecture and between Ohara and Onjuku in the Chiba Prefecture. Shirahama Beach on the Izu Peninsula has a good beach break for surfing and is also nice for chilling out. Experienced surfers take the ferry from Tokyo to the island of Nijima. Great reef breaks are at Miyazaki in Kyushu and off Amami-Oshima island in the Kagoshima Prefecture.

You can't get lost at Mount Fuji: just follow the crowds

REGIONAL OVERVIEW

RUSSIA

CHINA

NORTH KOREA

SOUTH KOREA

Imperial culture meets high-end shopping

Nippon Kai (Sea of Japan)

CENTRAL JAPAN p.

Kanazawa

THE WEST p. 100

Kyōto

Okayama

Ōsaka

Hiroshima

Kitakyūshū

Fukuoka

Matsuyama

Nagasaki

Kumamoto

Kagoshima

Miyazaki

THE SOUTH p. 116

Discover hidden Japa[n] far from the tourist tra[il]

Smouldering volcanoes and tropical fish

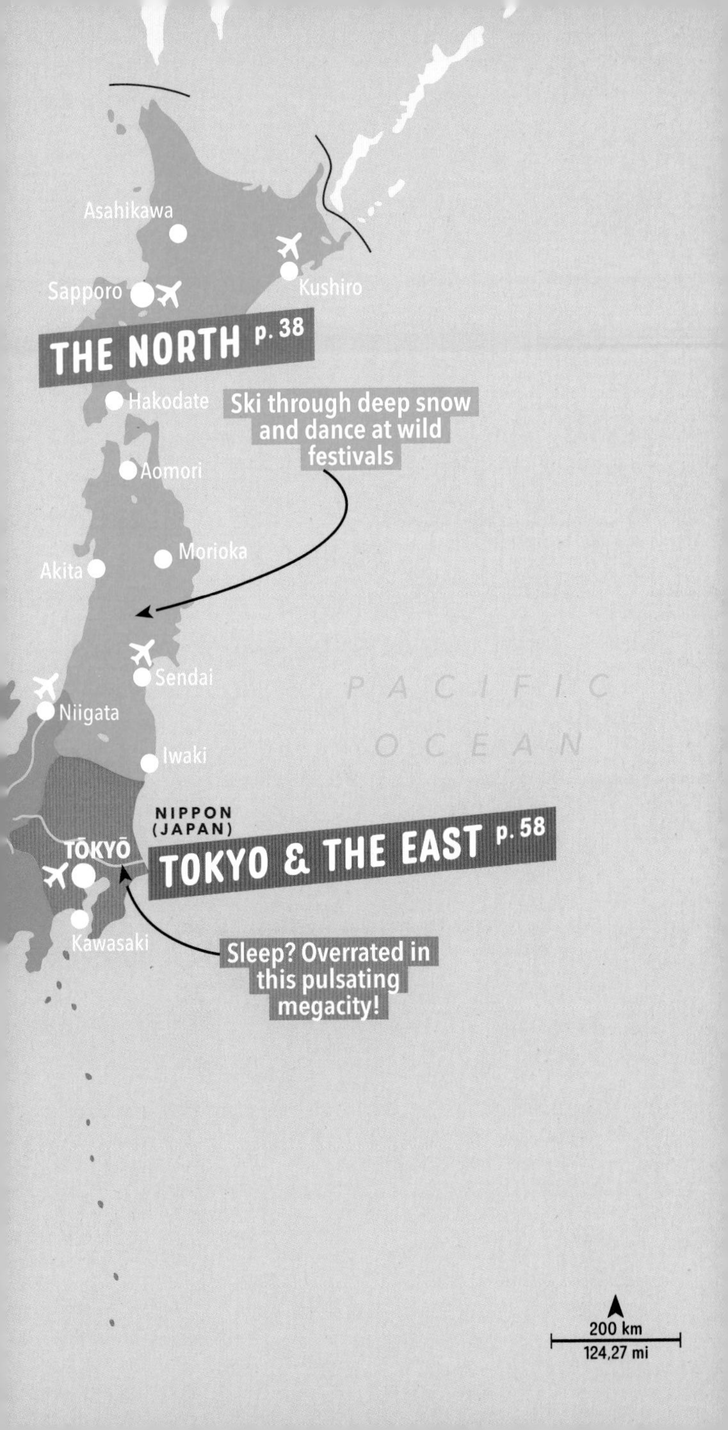

Asahikawa

Sapporo

Kushiro

THE NORTH p. 38

Hakodate

Ski through deep snow
and dance at wild
festivals

Aomori

Akita

Morioka

Sendai

Niigata

Iwaki

**NIPPON
(JAPAN)**

TŌKYŌ

TOKYO & THE EAST p. 58

Kawasaki

Sleep? Overrated in
this pulsating
megacity!

P A C I F I C

O C E A N

200 km
124,27 mi

THE NORTH

ANCIENT MYTHS & UNSPOILT NATURE

Wild bears and dancing orcas, holy mountains and dramatic coasts... Most travellers to Japan head west and south from Tokyo, thereby missing out on the rugged charm of the undeveloped north.

The northernmost island of Hokkaido – a little smaller than the island of Ireland – was the traditional homeland of the indigenous Ainu people who venerated bear gods. Since its annexation by Japan 150 years ago, Hokkaido has become a land of farms and vast fields

Refuge for the last of the samurai: Tsuruga Castle in Aizu-Wakamatsu

of vegetables and dairy cattle. The climate is continental European and the straight roads resemble those in the US.

Rocky coastline and forests characterise the unassuming region of Tohoku in the north-east of Honshu island. Here, farmers and fishermen tend their fields and fish for oysters. Since the quake, tsunami and nuclear catastrophe of 2011, Japan's north has focused on its core strengths: rustic hot springs, samurai traditions, wild festivals and unspoilt nature. Those who visit always want to return.

THE NORTH

Wakkanai 稚内市 ✈ 40
Rebun 礼文町
Rishiri 利尻町
Teshio 天塩町
Enbetsu 遠別町
Tomamae 苫前町
Obira 小平町
Mashike 増毛町
Sunagawa 砂川市

Shakotan 積丹町
Otaru 1
Sapporo Snow Festival ★
Sapporo p.42

Suttsu-Town 寿都町
2 **Niseko ★**
310km, 3¾ hrs 🚄
Date 伊達市
Setana せたな町
Yakumo 八雲町
Okushiri 奥尻島 ✈
Shikabe 鹿部町
Kaminokuni 上ノ国町
Hakodate p.47

Matsumae 松前町
Oma 大間町
Mutsu むつ市
Imabetsu 今別町 ✈
Yokohama 横浜町
JR Gono Line ★ 6
Aomori p.48
Ajigasawa 鰺ヶ沢町
Fukaura 深浦町
5 Towada-Hachimantai-Nationalpark
Shirakami Sanchi 7
Happo 八峰町
Hirosaki 弘前市
Kitaakita 北秋田市
45
360km, 1 hr 52mins 🚄
Oga 男鹿市
Morioka p.50
Akita 秋田市
Kakunodate samurai houses ★ 10
Sanriku-Fukko-Nationalpark 8
Hanamaki 花巻市
9 Tono
Yokote 横手市
Nikaho にかほ市
Chuson-ji ★ 11
12 Geibikei-Schlucht
Sakata 酒田市
Tsuruoka 鶴岡市
Osaki 大崎市
Matsushima ★ 13
Murakami 村上市
Yamadera 15
Sado 佐渡市 ✈
Niigata 新潟市
Schneemonster von Zao 14
45
Shibata 新発田市
Sendai p.52
7
160km, 2 hrs 10mins 🚄
Sanjo 三条市
Fukushima 福島市
49
Suzu 珠洲市
Nagaoka 長岡市
Wajima 輪島市
Ouchi-Juku 16
Aizu-Wakamatsu ★ p.56

Nippon Kai

Tomakomai 苫小牧市

Esashi 枝幸町
Omu 雄武町
Okoppe 興部町
Monbetsu 紋別市
Takinoue 滝上町
Yubetsu 湧別町
Kamikawa 上川町
30 km, 4½ hrs
Shintoku 新得町

RUSSIA РОССИЯ

Shiretoko National Park★ p. 46

3 Drift Ice Watching
4 Abashiri-Gefängnismuseum
Kitami 北見市
Shibetsu 標津町
Teshikaga 弟子屈町
Betsukai 別海町
44
Ashoro 足寄町
Nemuro 根室市
Hamanaka 浜中町
Obihiro 帯広市
Urahoro 浦幌町
Kushiro 釧路市
Urakawa 浦河町
Taiki 大樹町
Hiroo 広尾町
Erimo えりも町

PACIFIC

OCEAN

100 km
62.14 mi

MARCO POLO HIGHLIGHTS

★ **SAPPORO SNOW FESTIVAL**
Never mind snowmen: these snow sculptures of famous buildings from around the world are true works of art ➤ p. 45

★ **NISEKO**
The best region for deep snow skiing in Japan ➤ p. 45

★ **SHIRETOKO NATIONAL PARK**
Hike in this UNESCO World Heritage Site, watch bears catching salmon and look out for orcas ➤ p. 46

★ **JR GONO LINE**
Travel for hours on this cosy slow train and enjoy views of the sea and ancient birch forest ➤ p. 50

★ **KAKUNODATE SAMURAI HOUSES**
You might meet samurais and geishas at any minute… ➤ p. 52

★ **CHUSON-JI**
Unbelievable craftsmanship in a temple in Hiraizumi which has lasted for 900 years ➤ p. 54

★ **MATSUSHIMA**
Whether raw or grilled, here you can try oysters straight from the sea ➤ p. 55

★ **AIZU-WAKAMATSU**
Breathtaking black-and-red lacquerware from the old samurai city ➤ p. 56

SAPPORO

(▨ H3) **Whether you like beer, grilled lamb and large crabs, or are looking for a break from the humid summer weather, or love to ski or snowboard, then the host city of the 1972 Winter Olympics is the place to be.**

From here, it is not far to several ski regions with sought-after powder snow. For the snow festival in early February, Sapporo displays huge, illuminated snow sculptures. Navigating the city should be easy because Japan's fifth-biggest metropolis (pop. 1.97 million) is laid out in a grid like a chess board.

SIGHTSEEING

MOERENUMA PARK
(モエレ沼公園)

Sculptor and landscape designer Isamu Noguchi inspired this municipal park on a former landfill site that

WHERE TO START?

Many buses and trains depart from the **main station** and from nearby Odori Park, which stretches through the city centre like a green ribbon. Numerous sights can be reached by hopping on the Sapporo Shiden tram from Nishiyonchome station next to the park *(from 200 yen, or with the Dosanko pass for 360 yen/day at weekends)*.

was completed in 2013. You can hire a bicycle and ride along geometrically laid-out paths around a conical hill, past sculptures and a glass pyramid *(end of April to early Nov | 100 yen/hr). Daily 7am–10pm except for 1–3 Jan | admission free | Moerenuma-koen 1-1, Higashi-ku |* 東区モエレ沼公園1-1 *| Moerenuma-Koen bus station Higashiguchi (east entrance) | moerenumapark.jp |* ⏱ *1–1½ hrs*

INSIDER TIP
Sightseeing for sporty types

SAPPORO BEER MUSEUM
(サッポロビール博物館)

Munich, Sapporo and Milwaukee, the three "alcohol capitals" of the world, are at the same latitude? Wrong! This myth was spread by an advertisement for the Sapporo beer brand. Founded in 1876, Japan's oldest brewery is regarded as one of the best. After a short guided tour, including beer tasting, you can grill lamb à la Genghis Khan at your table in the *Garden Grill. Daily 11am–8pm | admission free | Higashi 9-1-1, Kita 7-jo, Higashi-ku |* 東区北7条東9-1-1 *| sapporobeer. jp | Sapporo Beer-en bus station*

SAPPORO CLOCK TOWER
(札幌市時計台)

In the past, students of the agricultural college were taught in today's clock tower, which was renovated in 2018/19. The clock, which dates from 1881, was manufactured in Massachusetts and has been the symbol for the historical and cultural development of Sapporo ever since. A brief photo stop should be sufficient

Sapporo Snow Festival: view the white delight from the TV tower

to do this Sapporo landmark justice. *Daily 8.45am–5.10pm | admission 200 yen | 2-chome Kita 1 Jonishi, Chuo-ku* | 市中央区北1条西2丁目 | *Sapporo railway station | sapporo-shi-tokeidai.jp/english*

MOIWA (藻岩山)

This wooded mountain south-west of Sapporo offers breathtaking views. In the evening, the city lights sparkle like stars as far as the Sea of Japan. The ride to the viewing platform including restaurant and planetarium – initially by ropeway, then by a mini-cable car – is all part of the fun. *Daily 11am–10pm | ride 1,700 yen, children 850 yen | tram to Iriguchi ropeway station, shuttle bus to the ropeway and mini-cable car | Chuo-ku, Fushimi 5-3-7* | 中央区伏見5-3-7 | *sapporo.travel*

EATING & DRINKING

SOUP CALYI PICANTE (スープカリィピカンティ)

The people of Hokkaido love soup curry with lots of fresh vegetables and spices. Try a bowl of this soul food and never have cold feet again! *Daily 11.30am–11pm | Acroview Hokudaimae, Kita 13, Jonishi 3-2-23, Kita-ku* | 北区北十三条西3-2-23アクロビュー北大前 | *picante.jp | ¥*

SATURDAY'S CHOCOLATE FACTORY CAFE (サタデイズ チョコレート ファクトリー カフェ)

Crafted by hand from the bean to the table as well as creatively packed. Chocolate fans simply have to try a hot chocolate, frozen chocolate shake *and* brownies. *Thu–Tue 10am–6.30pm | Chuo-ku, Minami 2 Johigashi 2-7-1*

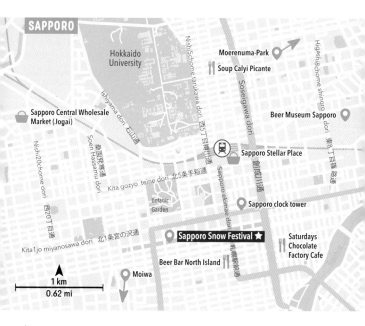

SAPPORO

Hokkaido University

Moerenuma-Park

Soup Calyi Picante

Sapporo Central Wholesale Market (Jogai)

Beer Museum Sapporo

Sapporo Stellar Place

Nishi3chome sarukawa dori 西5丁目樽川通

Ishiyama dori 石山通

Soen Hassamu dori 蔡園琴薩夢通

Kita gozyo teine dori 北5条手稲通

Botanic Garden

Kita1jo miyanosawa dori 北1条宮の沢通

1 km
0.62 mi

Moiwa

Beer Bar North Island

Soseigawa dori 創成川通

Sapporo ekimae dori 札幌駅前通

Sapporo clock tower

Sapporo Snow Festival ★

札幌駅前通

Saturdays Chocolate Factory Cafe

Higashi8chome shinorg 東8丁目稲影通

Nishi20chome dori 西20丁目

Salmon Bldg., 1F | 中央区南2条東
2丁目7-1 Salmon 1F ビル |
saturdayschocolate.com | ¥

SHOPPING

SAPPORO STELLAR PLACE
(札幌ステラプレイス)

If you can't find it here, you won't find
it anywhere: the shopping mall at the
southern entrance of Sapporo railway
station is one of the biggest in Japan.
It has 200 shops and many restaurants (open until 11pm) serving
Hokkaido cuisine at affordable prices.
Treat yourself to a massage, manicure
or visit to the cinema. *Daily 10am–9pm
depending on the shop | Chuo-ku, Kita
5 Jonishi 2-chome* | 中央区北5条西
2丁目 | *uu-hokkaido.in/corporate/
buy/sapporo/stellarplace.shtml*

SAPPORO CENTRAL WHOLESALE
MARKET (JOGAI) (札幌市中央
卸売市場 場外市場)

This experience requires an early start.
Have you ever seen crabs with up to
50-cm-long legs? From 6am the salespeople shout about their wares in the
wholesale market's outer area *(jogai)*
which is also open to visitors. You can
taste snacks for free or enjoy freshly
caught fish. *Daily 6am–5pm | Chuo-ku,
Kita 11 Jonishi 21-2-3* | 中央区北11
条西21丁目21-2-3 | *Nijuyonken rail-
way station, Tozai line*

SPORT & ACTIVITIES

SAPPORO OLYMPIC MUSEUM
(札幌オリンピックミュージア
ム)

A chairlift takes you to the ski jump

that was built for the Sapporo Winter Olympics 1972 – with panoramic views of the city. In the museum you can take a virtual jump in a simulator, go cross-country skiing or dare to try a virtual run in a four-man bob-sleigh at 130kmh. *May–Oct daily 9am–6pm, Nov–April daily 9.30am–5pm | admission 600 yen, children free, chairlift 500 yen, children (up to age 12) 300 yen | 1274 Miyanomori, Chuo-ku |* 中央区宮の森*1274 | 10 mins by taxi from Maruyama Koen railway station | sapporo-olympicmuseum.jp/english |* 🕐 *2 hrs*

INSIDER TIP
Feel like an Olympian

FESTIVALS

SAPPORO SNOW FESTIVAL
(札幌雪まつり) ★
An extraordinary and spectacular winter festival! The British Museum and the Pyramids of Giza, among many others, have all been formed out of snow in Sapporo. From humble beginnings with students creating statues in the 1950s, this festival today boasts more than 100 gigantic artworks, attracting more than 2 million visitors who can enjoy the illuminated masterpieces until 10pm. Book your accommodation early! *1st/2nd week in February | snowfes.com/english*

NIGHTLIFE

BEER BAR NORTH ISLAND
(ビアバーノースアイランド)
With twelve varieties of craft beer fresh from the keg every day, it will

take some time to try them all! How about a *Coriander Black* to start with? A rarity in Japan, smoking is banned in this beer pub with its tiled walls and wooden bar stools. *Mon–Sat 6pm–midnight, Sun 3–10pm | Chuo-ku, Minami 2 Jonishi, 4-10-1, Large Country Building 10F |* 中央区南2条西4-10-1　ラージカントリービル 10F *| northislandbeer.jp/bar.html | ¥*

AROUND SAPPORO

1 OTARU (小樽市)
30km from Sapporo / 45 mins by train
This port city (pop. 118,000) is a popular day trip destination for the people of Sapporo. Can you hear German beerhall music coming from one of the old warehouses by the Otaru canal? This houses the *Otaru Beer* microbrewery *(April–Oct daily 11am–11pm, Nov–March until 10pm | Minatomachi 5-4 |* 港町*5-4)*, which is run by a German brewer. It also serves typical German food. 🗺 *H3*

2 NISEKO (ニセコ町) ★
90km from Sapporo / 3 hrs by bus
Australians love this ski resort for its reliable snow cover and the "best powder snow in the world". Niseko (pop. 5,200) consists of four ski resorts with 70 slopes *(niseko.ne.jp)*. The *Niseko Grand Hirafu* ski region allows you to ski until 8.30pm, followed by après-ski. *Niseko Annapuri* is also suitable

for beginners and for those who prefer a quieter atmosphere. *H3*

SHIRETOKO NATIONAL PARK

(*K2*) **This is as remote as it gets! The ⭐ Shiretoko Peninsula in the far north-west of Hokkaido is a UNESCO World Heritage Site.**

Although it's largely accessible only on foot or by boat, the national park is a must-visit for nature lovers. The resident brown bears are best watched

Mt. Rausu is a great hiking destination on Shiretoko

from the water. The centre of the densely forested peninsula is covered by a mountain range, including the 1,665-m-high Mount Rausu. You can reach its peak on an arduous but popular hike. Many hikers fix little bells to their backpacks to warn off the bears, although these shy animals are unlikely to approach humans. The islands off Shiretoko are inaccessible: although claimed by Japan, Russia has kept them occupied since the end of World War II.

SIGHTSEEING

FIVE LAKES (知床五湖)

An easy hike leads round the idyllic lakes of Shiretoko Goko, which mirror the mountain range in their still waters. In 90 minutes you can walk around all five lakes, while 40 minutes are sufficient to circumnavigate two of them. From a wooden walkway above a sea of bamboo grass you can see the Sea of Okhotsk. *Park open end of April–end of Nov, during peak season (10 May–31 July) hiking is only allowed with a guide (approx. 5,000 yen), booking recommended | goko.go.jp/fivelakes/?locale=en*

BEAR WATCHING 🐻

An adventure on the northern side of Shiretoko: watch bears catching salmon in the river from the safety of your boat. At approx. 3,000 animals, this is Japan's largest wild population of brown bears. *28 April–25 Oct 6 short tours from Utoro daily (1½ hrs | 3,100 yen) and 2 long tours (3¾ hrs | 6,500 yen) | ms-aurora.com/shiretoko/en*

WHALE WATCHING 🐳

Sperm whales, orcas, dolphins and seals gather on the southern side of Shiretoko near Rausu harbour. Take your camera! *May–Oct 2–3 tours daily | 8,000 yen/2½ hrs | e-shiretoko.com/howtobooking.html*

AROUND SHIRETEKO NATIONAL PARK

❸ DRIFT ICE WATCHING
(流氷観光砕氷船おーろら)
75km from Utoro in Shiretoko / 1 hr and 20 mins by car

Shiretoko is the most southerly location in the northern hemisphere where one can see drift ice. The icebreaker *Aurora* departs from Abashiri harbour *(20 Jan–3 April 2–5 tours daily | 3,300 yen/hr | ms-aurora.com/abashiri/en)*. Alternatively, from Rausu harbour *(daily Feb–March | 4,000 yen/hr, 10,000 yen/2½ hrs)*. 📖 *J2*

❹ ABASHIRI PRISON MUSEUM
(網走刑務所)
80km from Utoro in Shiretoko /1 hr and 25 mins by car

Abashiri, founded 100 years ago, was Japan's Alcatraz. Those who were spared the death sentence were sent to the coldest point at the northern end of the country. Today you can walk through the corridors of the prison, which has been turned into an outdoor museum. It is the world's oldest and biggest prison made of wood. The building's posts and wooden ceilings were made from trees which the inmates themselves had to cut and carve. The former prison canteen now serves original menus made of rice, fish, vegetables and miso soup *(11am–3.30pm). Daily May–Sept 8.30am–6pm, Oct–April 9am–5pm | admission 1,080 yen | 1-1 Aza Yobito, Abashiri | 網走市字呼人1-1 | kangoku.jp/multilingual_english/index.html |* ⏱ *1½ hrs |* 📖 *J2*

INSIDER TIP
Enjoy a prisoner's lunch

HAKODATE

(📖 H4) **This charming port city in the south of Hokkaido (pop. 259,000) is known for the spectacular panoramic views from Mount Hakodate, which can be reached by cable car, and for the Motomachi quarter on its slopes.**

In 1859, Hakodate was one of the first ports to open to foreign traders, and it shows to this day because European, American and Russian influences merge with the Japanese culture. Since 2016 the city, which was hard to reach in the past, has been accessible from Tokyo by Shinkansen bullet train in four hours.

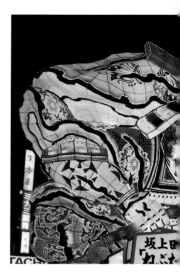

SIGHTSEEING

GORYOKAKU (五稜郭)

The view from the 107-m-tall Goryokaku Tower explains why this imposing 18th-century fortress, which is now a park, is unique in Japan: it is star-shaped! The fortress ditch is planted with cherry trees which burst into bright pink blossom in spring, while in the autumn the fortress is covered in yellow and red leaves. *Daily 8am–7pm, 21 Oct–20 April 9am–6pm | tower admission 900 yen | 43-9 Goryokaku-cho | 五稜郭町43-9 | Goryokaku Koen Iriguchi bus station*

SHOPPING

HAKODATE MORNING MARKET (函館朝市) 🐟

Next to the railway station, market traders serve fresh seafood. You can pull octopus, the local speciality, from the tank yourself and have it prepared as a personalised sashimi. *Daily 6am–2pm, May–Dec from 5am | 9-19 Wakamatsucho | 若松町9-19 | JR station Hakodate*

INSIDER TIP
Catch your sashimi

AOMORI

(⊞ H4) **The port promenade of Aomori (pop. 282,000) is dominated by a gigantic glass pyramid where you can get countless varieties of the city's speciality: apples.**

The name Aomori means "green forest", and the capital of the prefecture of the same name is indeed a centre of forestry and fishery. Situated in the Bay of Mutsu, the city's structure from the Edo period has been largely retained despite bombing in World War II, but sadly the buildings themselves didn't survive. Up until the opening of the Seikan underwater tunnel in 1988, ferries to Hokkaido departed from Aomori. Now that the ferries have gone, the city has become much quieter, except during the *Nebuta Matsuri* festival in summer.

SIGHTSEEING

NEBUTA MUSEUM WA RASSE (ねぶたの家 ワ・ラッセ) 🌂

This museum is a work of art in itself: the building is constructed from a 12-m-tall curtain of vertical, red steel beams. Inside, several original Nebuta festival floats bring to life the spirit of

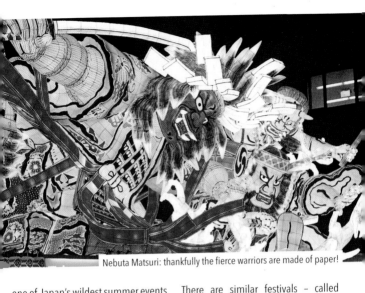
Nebuta Matsuri: thankfully the fierce warriors are made of paper!

one of Japan's wildest summer events. *Daily May–Aug 9am–7pm, Sept–April 9am–6pm, closed 31 Dec/1 Jan, 9/10 Aug | admission 600 yen | 1-1-1 Yasukata | 安方1-1-1 | 1 min on foot from JR station Aomori | ⏱ 1–1½ hrs*

FESTIVALS

NEBUTA MATSURI 🚩

All hell breaks loose in otherwise quiet Aomori in the first week of August: dancers pull 20 floats through the city's streets, décorated with enormous illuminated and colourful paper lanterns, many of whichh display historical warriors in battle. They are accompanied by the sounds of thundering drums and piercing flutes. You can hire the right outfit in town – a cotton kimono with a special printed pattern *(yukata)*, a yellow belt and red ribbons – and join the dance *(hire fee 4,000 yen, purchase price 7,000 yen).*

There are similar festivals – called *Neputa Matsuri* – in Hirosaki *(1–7 Aug)* and Goshogawara *(4–8 Aug)*. Definitely book your accommodation early!

AROUND AOMORI

5 TOWADA HACHIMANTAI NATIONAL PARK
(十和田八幡平国立公園)
70km from Aomori / 3 hrs by train
In October, the shores of Lake Towada-ko, the biggest caldera on the main island of Honshu, explodes into a riot of coloured leaves in all shades from bright yellow to deep red. A pleasant way to explore the lake is by sightseeing boat from Yasumiya and Nenokuchi *(duration 50 mins, but not in winter)*. On Mount Hakkoda the

leaves change colour as early as late September. JR buses run between Aomori, Hakkoda and the lake *(3,090 yen)*. □ *H4*

6 JR GONO LINE (五能線) ★
34km from Aomori / 40 mins to Kawabe by train

The scenic railway between Kawabe and Higashi-Noshiro (150km) allows

the habitat of the Asian black bear, black woodpecker and Japanese serow – a goat-like mammal. Today, 170km² remain of an unspoilt birch forest that was once the largest in East Asia. From the castle city of Hirosaki you can go on a beautiful half- or full-day hike through the forest. Calculate between two to three hours for the popular return route to the three

Making a cast-iron teapot requires time and patience

you to get comfortable, listen to traditional live music or just admire the scenery: the Sea of Japan and the birch forest. The journey is wonderful at sunset! *Trains may not always run in winter. Booking required. The JR Rail Pass is valid on this train.* | □ *G4*

7 SHIRAKAMI SANCHI (白神山地)
60km from Aomori / 75 mins by car
This UNESCO World Heritage Site is

Anmon waterfalls *(8km | end of April– end of Nov)*. □ *G4*

MORIOKA

(□ H5) **Located on the banks of three rivers, the capital (pop. 292,000) of Iwate is set in attractive countryside, surrounded by mountains.**

The city features several historic buildings and temples as well as castle ruins. A heavy, but durable and popular, souvenir from Morioka is a cast-iron teapot *(nambu tetsubin)*, although you may find the turned and painted wooden dolls *(kokeshi)* easier to pack in your suitcase.

SIGHTSEEING

HOON-JI TEMPLE (報恩寺)

It took nine artisans from Kyoto five years to carve 499 wooden Buddhist statues in the 300-year old Hoon-ji temple. **Who's who?** Can you spot the images of Marco Polo and Kublai Khan, a grandson of Genghis Khan? *Daily 9am–4pm | admission 300 yen | 31-5 Nasukawa-chome | 名須川町31-5 | 10 mins by taxi from JR station Morioka*

EATING & DRINKING

AZUMAYA (東家)

This traditional restaurant at the railway station focuses on food rather than drinks. Sit on tatami rice straw mats to eat *wanko soba*, which is more of an all-you-can-eat challenge than a culinary delight. This is because each portion consists of only a few bites of soba buckwheat noodles; as soon as you have finished your plate, you are served the next one. Most women manage 30 to 40 bowls and men, 50 to 60, although the record is more than 600! *Daily 11am–3pm, 5–8pm | 8-11 Moriokaekimaedori | 盛岡駅前通り8-11 | JR station Morioka | ¥*

SHOPPING

IWACHU (岩鋳)

Tea served from iron pots tastes milder, and the pots are decorative as well. At Iwachu you can watch the masters at work and choose between traditional and modern designs in their shop. *Daily 8.30am–5.30pm | 2-23-9 Minamisenboku | 南仙北 2-23-9 | 15 mins by taxi from JR station Morioka*

AROUND MORIOKA

8 SANRIKU FUKKO NATIONAL PARK (三陸復興国立公園)

90km from Morioka / 1¾ hrs to Miyako by hire car

A rugged and beautiful rocky coastline with tiny islands offshore, wind-blown cedars and many small fishing villages – this is the narrowest national park in Japan. It stretches for several hundred kilometres along the eastern Pacific coast and includes the region that was destroyed by the tsunami, which followed the catastrophic earthquake in 2011. However, nature is resilient: for example, between Taro and Miyako is the idyllic beach of Jodogahama which, with its jagged pine trees contorted by the wind and bare rocks, is the perfect photo opportunity – this is how people think of Japan! It is best to explore the region by hire car, although there are some bus and train services too. In many locations, witnesses of the disaster offer guided tours by taxi or bus. If you have some time to spare und love hiking, check out the 900-km long Michinoku Coastal Trail in the park *(tohoku.env.go.jp/mct/english)*, see also Discovery Tour No.3. *H5*

⑨ TONO (遠野市)

80km from Morioka / 2 hrs by bus

This farming town (pop. 27,000) in the mountains of Kitakami is known throughout the country for the *Tono Monogatari* collection of fairy tales from this area, for example of the water spirit Kappa who looks like a grumpy frog in human form carrying a tortoise shell. In Tono you will find many of these figurines. This agricultural region is also known for traditional farmhouses with thatched roofs which you can admire in the pretty outdoor museum of *Tono Denshoen (daily 9am–5pm | admission 320 yen | 6 Chiwari-5-1 Tsuchibuchicho Tsuchibuchi | 30 mins by hire bicycle from Tono railway station, 10 mins by taxi).* Take off your shoes and have a look inside! *H5*

⑩ KAKUNODATE SAMURAI HOUSES (角館武家屋敷) ★

65km from Morioka / 45 mins by train

There are few locations in Japan where you get the feeling that a samurai or geisha could come round the corner any minute. The former samurai hotspot of Akita has dozens of well-preserved traditional samurai houses, which you may want to see in a rickshaw because the drivers don't just know the best spots but also have

a good sense of humour. Kakunodate is usually quiet; at the end of April or in early May when hundreds of cherry trees are blossoming, it can become a little overcrowded – but it's always beautiful. *Daily 9am–5pm (in winter until 4pm) | Senboku-shi, Kakunodatemachi Bukeyashiki-dori |* 仙北市角館町武家屋敷通り *| kakunodate-kanko.jp/language/en/ kakunodate | 15 mins on foot from Kakunodate railway station |* *H5*

SENDAI

(H6) **Expansive, green and modern – Sendai (pop. 1.1 million), the capital of the Miyagi Prefecture, is the perfect starting point for tours to the country's north-east.**

The city itself has a lot to offer. Its nickname "city of trees" is due to a wide avenue with tall Japanese zelkovas, an elm species, in its centre. The city's many educational institutions, such as the renowned Tohoku University, give it a lively student atmosphere. The climate is pleasant: not too hot in summer and not too cold in winter.

SIGHTSEEING

ZUIHODEN (瑞鳳殿)

When Sendai's feudal lord, Masamune Date, died in 1636, his family had a grand mausoleum constructed for him, with colourful woodcarvings and a lot of gold leaf on a black backdrop. This exceptional building is awesome.

Daily Feb–Nov 9am–4.30pm, Dec–Jan until 4pm, closed New Year's Eve | admission 550 yen | 23-2 Otamayashita, Aoba-ku | 青葉区霊屋下23-2 | Loople Sendai bus station Zuihoden-mae | zuihoden.com/en

RINNOJI (輪王寺)

At first sight this Buddhist temple is rather unremarkable, but its garden is idyllic and traditional! Koi carp circle in the pond, the trees have been clipped into a perfect shape, and behind it all a three-storey pagoda reaches for the sky. The temple has a long history: founded in 1441 in another location, it was eventually relocated to the north of the city – in order to protect the city from a cardinal direction that was regarded as particularly inauspicious. *Daily 8am–5pm |* *admission 300 yen | 1-14-1 Kitayama, Aoba-ku | 青葉区北山1-14-1 | JR station Kitayama*

EATING, DRINKING & SHOPPING

Sendai is famous throughout Japan for two specialities: a tender piece of grilled beef tongue known as *gyutan* and sweets made from pureed green soy beans *(zunda)* which are also delicious as a shake.

GYUTAN FUKUSUKE HONTEN (牛たん福助本店)

Only a three-minute walk from the west entrance of the JR railway station of Sendai, this restaurant has been serving beef tongue for 40 years, both grilled and as a *shabushabu* meat

LIFE ON THE COAST AFTER THE TSUNAMI

A dozen years after the megaquake on 11 March 2011, which devastated the Fukushima nuclear power plant, memories of the dreadful event are slowly fading. At the time, a house-height tsunami devastated hundreds of kilometres of coastline *(*⌂ *H6)*, leaving 18,500 dead in the region of Tohoku. However, despite the trauma of 2011, the locals show resilience.

As a warning to future generations, the Taro Kanko Hotel in Taro has been kept as a ruin, with only the beams of the lower floors left intact. In Rikuzentakata, you can see a block of flats where the tsunami crushed all balconies and windows up to the fourth floor. In Minamisanriku, the metal skeleton of the former disaster protection centre points to the sky. When the tsunami approached, 53 people sought refuge on its flat roof, but only 10 managed not to be swept away. There are countless stories of this kind.

In the years following the tsunami, the debris was gradually removed, and factories and settlements were rebuilt step by step. In Onagawa, the symbol for this new beginning is a shopping street by the railway station where, at the entrance, you can dip your feet into hot spring water.

fondue. The ambience is westernised to modern. *Wed–Mon 11.30am–2pm and 5–11pm | Aoba-ku, 1-8-24 Chuo Lovely, KK Bldg. 2F |* 青葉区中央 1-8-24 ラブリーKKビル2F | ¥¥

TAMAZAWA SOUHONTEN
(玉澤総本店)

Japanese sweets are less sweet then those in Europe and often consist of sweet beans and soft *mochi* (rice cakes). In this shop in the *S-PAL* shopping mall you can taste a particularly large variety of sweet delights, for example numerous varieties with green soy bean puree. Sit at the counter and watch how the tea is prepared. *Daily shop 9am–9pm, café 9am–8pm | 1-1-1 Chuo, Aoba-ku |* 青葉区中央 1-1-1 | *JR station Sendai*

FESTIVALS

SENDAI TANABATA MATSURI
(仙台七夕まつり)

Tanabata star festivals are held in many places in the country in July and August. According to a Chinese legend, the two stars Vega and Altair, who represent two lovers, only meet on one day each year. Sendai hosts a particularly big and colourful festival from 6 to 8 August. The shopping streets in the city centre are decorated with joyful paper flags that float from long bamboo poles. Numerous events take place on the side. *sendaitanabata.com/en*

JOZENJI STREET JAZZ FESTIVAL
(定禅寺ストリートジャズフェスティバル)

In September, Sendai hosts a weekend jazz festival. From morning to evening, on every street corner, hundreds of bands, artists and orchestras, from amateur musicians to professionals, give it their all. *j-street jazz.com/language/english.html*

NIGHTLIFE

KOKUBUNCHO (国分町)

The biggest night-time quarter in the north-east of the country has everything from tiny bars with counters and cosy *izakaya* pubs, to restaurants with international cuisine to nightclubs and red-light establishments. There are 3,000 restaurants between Jozenji-dori and Hirose-dori streets alone, catering for every taste and budget.

AROUND SENDAI

🎇 CHUSON-JI ⭐ 🚩
100km from Sendai / 45 mins by train

A visit to the extensive temple complex in Hiraizumi, surrounded by both broadleaf and conifer forests, is like time-travelling back to the Heian period. The Konjikido Hall, its roof entirely covered in gold leaf, is an incredible 900 years old and has been declared a UNESCO World Heritage Site. *Daily March–Oct 8.30am–5pm, Nov–Feb 8.30am–4.30pm | admission 800 yen | 202 Koromonoseki, Hiraizumi |* 平泉町平泉衣関202 |

25 mins on foot from Hiraizumi railway station | ⏱ 2 hrs | 🗺 H5

12 GEIBIKEI GORGE (猊鼻渓)
120km from Sendai / 75 mins by train

This 2km-long, picturesque gorge (not to be confused with the Genbikei Gorge) is best explored on a comforta-

INSIDER TIP
Warm your-self on the inside

ble 90-minute boat tour, and the skipper will even sing for you. In winter the crew serves hot soup on the journey. *Daily April–Aug 8.30am–4.30pm, Sept–Oct 8.30am–4pm, Nov–March 9am–3pm | tickets 1,500 yen | 467 Nagasaka Azamachi, Higashiyama-cho, Ichinoseki |* 関市東山町長坂字町467 *| JR station Geibikei | f H5*

13 MATSUSHIMA (松島) ★
27km from Sendai / 25 mins by train

In the town of Matsushima everything is about oysters! You can find numerous varieties of this delicious seafood in the fish market – they're even served as a burger. The Bay of Matsushima, with its 260 pine-covered islets, is regarded as one of the three most beautiful in the whole of Japan. On a boat tour of the bay, the seagulls will feed from your hand. To warm yourself up, you can have a bowl of oyster stew *(kaki nabe)* on the boat. *Various operators | daily 10am–4pm, in winter until 3pm from Matsushima, from 9am from Shiogama | duration 25–50 mins | ticket 1,000–1,500 yen | marubun-kisen.com/english | 🗺 H6*

14 SNOW MONSTERS OF ZAO (蔵王の樹氷) 👹
90km from Sendai / 2 hrs by bus

Every year, the village of Zao falls victim to "snow monsters" *(juhyo)* when cold air laden with moisture sweeps

Walk across to a tiny island in Matsushima Bay

The "Snow Monsters" of Zao

across from Russia. The air is trapped by Mount Kumano (1,841m) and frozen water droplets cover the mountain's conifers with a thick layer of snow and ice. It can be an extraordinary sight as nature creates icy creatures that look like a horde of frozen Godzillas! *Two direct tours every day mid-Dec–mid-March | for bookings phone 0224 85 30 55 | tickets 4,800–6,800 yen | "Juhyo-go" bus from JR station Sendai, end of the village, exit at Sumikawa Snow Park | zaospa.or.jp/english | ▢ H6*

15 YAMADERA (山寺)

70km from Sendai / 65 mins by train
First you climb 1,000 steps and then you have to come down again, but it's worth the effort because the peak of Mount Yamadera rewards you with a marvellous 360-degree view of the wooded mountains of Yamagata. Back at the foot of the mountain, have a look into the Konponchu-do Hall where a ritual flame is said to have burnt continuously since the temple was founded in AD 860 CE. *Thu–Tue April–Nov 9.30am–4pm, Dec–March 10am–3.30pm | admission 300 yen | 4456-1 Yamadera, Yamagata-shi | 山形市山寺4456-1 | Yamadera railway station (Senzan line) | ▢ H6*

INSIDER TIP
Eternal flame

AIZU-WAKAMATSU

(▢ G6) **The proud samurai and castle city of ★ Aizu-Wakamatsu (pop. 120,000) lies just 120km west of the Fukushima Daiichi nuclear power plant that was destroyed in 2011.**

But its inland position, surrounded by mountains, meant that little of the released radioactivity reached the city. It has been a centre for the manufacture of red-and-black lacquerware for centuries; today, modern designs are produced as well, for example on glass. The region also produces rice wine that is appreciated throughout Japan.

SIGHTSEEING

TSURUGA CASTLE (鶴ヶ城)

For centuries, this towering castle was the most powerful fortress in northeast Japan. During the Boshin War, the last of the samurai retreated there, and as a result the castle, a symbol of feudalism, was destroyed in 1874. It was rebuilt as a museum in 1965. Recent renovation work has given it back its original red roofing tiles. Daily 8.30am–5pm | admission 410 yen | samurai-city.jp/en | Tsurugajo Kitaguchi bus station | ⏱ 1 hr

SHOPPING

SUZUZEN (鈴善漆器店)

This lacquerware shop has been in business since the late 1500s! It sells both traditional items and modern interpretations of this old craft. If you book in advance, you can try your hand at decorating lacquerware with shiny powder in one of the 🐾 workshops. Daily 8.30am–5.30pm | workshop adults 1,300 yen, children 1,000 yen | 1-3-28 Chuo | 中央1-3-28 | Aizu-Wakamatsu railway station | suzuzen.com

AROUND AIZU-WAKAMATSU

16 OUCHI-JUKU (大内宿)
30km from Aizu-Wakamatsu / 2 hrs by train and bus

This tourist village is a must-visit! The former postal station enchants with its thatched houses, artisan workshops, restaurants and variety of accommodation. Try the buckwheat noodle soup *(soba)* and toasted rice cakes with miso. In winter it is simply idyllic! *Daily 9am–5pm | Ouchi, Shimogou, Minamiaizu |* 福島県南会津郡下郷町大字大内 *| Yunokami Onsen railway station, 15 mins by taxi |* 📖 G6

WHERE TO STAY IN THE NORTH

A ROMANTIC RYOKAN

In 🚩 *Mukaitaki (48 rooms | 200 Kawamukai, Oaza Yumoto, Higashiyama-machi | mukaitaki.jp | 20 mins by taxi from Aizu-Wakamatsu railway station | ¥ ¥ ¥)* you will sleep on tatami rice straw mats and futons in beautifully decorated rooms. In the evening, relax in the hot springs, hidden in a rambling building in the garden. This place is incredibly atmospheric, especially in winter when the inner garden is covered in snow and lit by lanterns.

TOKYO &
THE EAST

VAST & VARIED

What Paris is for France, the Kanto region in the east is for Japan. It is the focus for Japanese culture and business, and is home to a quarter of the country's population, most of whom live in the Greater Tokyo Area, one of the world's largest conurbations.

But don't be put off. The megacities of Tokyo and Yokohama are incredibly diverse; every district is different and distinct, and they're all interconnected by arguably the best railway network on earth.

Lanterns light the way to the Asakusa Kannon Temple

Tokyo is a top culinary destination, regularly awarded the most Michelin stars of any city on the planet. It's great for shopping, with a heady mix of traditional shopping streets and trendy malls. And it's safe and clean, without any no-go areas. The capital is also the perfect starting point for excursions: it takes only an hour by car to reach the ski resorts; the night-time ferry will transport you to the islands in the south, and in a couple of hours you can reach the mountains of Nikko where you'll find one of Japan's most beautiful temples.

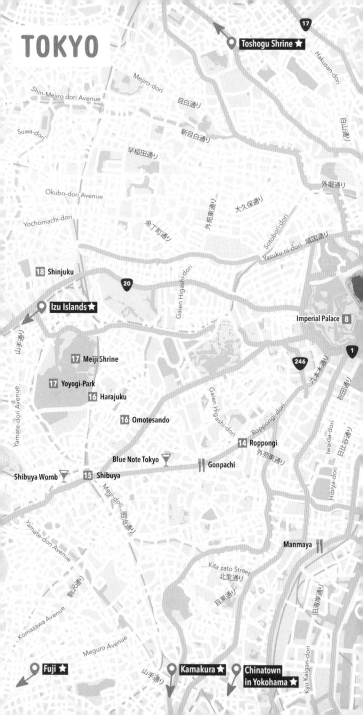

TOKYO

Toshogu Shrine ★ — 17

Hakusan-dori

Mejiro-dori
目白通り
Shin-Mejiro dori Avenue
新目白通り
Suwa-dori
早稲田通り
外堀通り
Okubo-dori Avenue
大久保通り
白山通り
Yochomachi-dori
余丁町通り
外苑東通り
Sotobori-dori
Yasukuni-dori 靖国通り

18 Shinjuku

20

Gaien Higashi-dori

Izu Islands ★

Imperial Palace 8

1

246

大木戸通り

17 Meiji Shrine

神田通り

17 Yoyogi-Park

16 Harajuku

Roppongi-dori

Iwaida-dori

Yamate-dori Avenue

16 Omotesando

Gaien Higashi-dori

14 Roppongi

外苑東通り

Blue Note Tokyo

Gonpachi

Hibiya-dori

Shibuya Womb   15 Shibuya

Meiji-dori 明治通り

Yamate-dori Avenue

Manmaya

Kita zato Street
北里通り

駒沢(R)通り

目黒通り

Komazawa Avenue

旧海岸通り

Meguro Avenue

Fuji ★

山手通り

Kamakura ★

Chinatown
in Yokohama ★

Kyu Kaigan-dori

6 Yanaka

4

6

Kokusai-dori

Kototoi-dori

言問通り

Meiji-dori

明治通り

Asakusa-Kannon Temple (Senso-ji) & 1
Asakusa Jinja Shrine

5 Ueno-Park

2 Tokyo Skytree ★

Asakusa-dori

浅草通り

国際通り

2K540 Aki Oka Artisan

Kuramaebashi-dori

蔵前橋通り

17

107

Akihabara 7 Shabushabu Onyasai

Kiyosumi-dori 清澄通り

Edo Tokyo Museum 4   3 Sumida Hokusai Museum

4

新大橋通り

Soranoiro Nippon

Shin-ohashi-dori

Kyukyudo

9 Ginza

Kabukiza-Theatre

Kiyosumi-dori 清澄通り

Fish market (Tsukiji) ★
10

11 Hamarikyu Onshi Teien

Harumi

Dori

明海通り

Amake-dori Avenue

有明通り

Port of Tokyo

Fish market (Toyosu) ★ 10

Mori Building Digital
Art Museum: teamLab
Borderless ★ 13

12 Odaiba

1 km
0.62 mi

MARCO POLO HIGHLIGHTS

★ **TOKYO SKYTREE**
Fabulous views over Tokyo and across to
Mount Fuji from the world's second-
tallest building ➤ p. 62

★ **FISH MARKET**
Come early to experience the biggest
fish market on earth ➤ p. 65

★ **MORI BUILDING DIGITAL ART
MUSEUM: TEAMLAB BORDERLESS**
Here you become both an artist and a
part of the artwork ➤ p. 66

★ **TOSHOGU SHRINE**
Breathe in history in Nikko, where
master craftsmen once worked ➤ p. 72

★ **CHINATOWN IN YOKOHAMA**
Taste China's cuisine with a Japanese
touch ➤ p. 74

★ **KAMAKURA**
This old imperial city is full of
unmissable sights – temples, shrines
and Buddhas ➤ p. 74

★ **FUJI**
Japan's iconic landmark: once seen,
never forgotten ➤ p. 76

★ **IZU ISLANDS**
Beaches, volcanoes and dolphins – and
only an hour's drive from Tokyo ➤ p. 77

TOKYO

(□ G7) **From the landmark 634-m-tall Tokyo Skytree, Japan's capital looks like an endless uniform mass of houses stretching to all sides, confined only by the Pacific Ocean and distant mountain ranges.**

Giant towers of concrete, glass and metal, a sea of light from advertising boards with their flashing lettering, flickering traffic lights, talking lifts and salespeople with megaphones – all this is Tokyo. But then you find yourself in a district that resembles a historic film set, where small terraced wooden houses with lacquered roofing tiles line up next to a temple, with a Shinto shrine around the corner. This idyllic village-like setting makes it hard to believe that the city centre is home to nine million people, that the Greater Tokyo Area has 12 million residents and that a total of 36 million live in the entire megalopolis.

Other districts will entice you into a shopping frenzy, visiting one cool

WHERE TO START?

At first, get an overview of the city from the world's second tallest building, the *Tokyo Skytree*. When you have seen enough of the urban jungle, move on to the nearby *Asakusa Shrine* and temple complex, but don't get lost in the *Nakamise-dori* shopping street which leads to these sanctuaries.

boutique after the other on the lookout for yet another fashionable item. There are many different Tokyos – go and find yours!

SIGHTSEEING

ASAKUSA KANNON TEMPLE (SENSO-JI) (浅草寺) & ASAKUSA JINJA SHRINE (浅草神社)

The Asakusa quarter was the heart of the old Edo capital. You can't miss Tokyo's most famous temple, the Senso-ji. First, you pass under the gigantic paper lantern of the "Thunder Gate" (*Kaminarimon*) and walk along the *Nakamise-dori* shopping street, where stalls sell baked *ningyoyaki* and fried *o-manju*: both are sweet bean puree cakes. Continue to an incense pot outside the temple. Copy the Japanese visitors and fan the incense to parts of your body that ache or where your hair is thinning. The smaller Asakusa Shrine nearby is dedicated to the fishermen who, in 628 CE, pulled a statue of Kannon, the Goddess of Mercy, from a river, thereby laying the foundation stone for the sanctuary. *Daily in summer 6am–5pm, winter 6.30am–5pm | 2-3-1 Asakusa, Taito-ku | 台東区浅草2-3-1 | tube G 19, A 18 Asakusa | ⏱ 1½ hrs | □ f1*

INSIDER TIP
If it helps, why not?

TOKYO SKYTREE (東京スカイツリー) ★

It is advisable to yawn or swallow to equalise the pressure in the super-fast lift that whisks you up one of the world's tallest towers. And while you

You will have to look long and hard to find Tokyo's wooden houses from the Skytree

may not reach the very top of this "tree in the sky", the view from its platforms at 350 and 450m is nevertheless sensational. On clear days you can even spot Mount Fuji more than 100km away. *Daily 8am–10pm | admission 2,000 yen (350m) or 3,000 yen (450m) | 1-1-13 Oshiage, Sumida-ku |* 墨田区押上1-1-13 *| subway A 20, Z 14 Oshiage | tokyo-skytree.jp/en |* ⏱ *1 hr |* 📖 *f1*

SUMIDA HOKUSAI MUSEUM (すみだ北斎美術館)

This newest addition to the city's collection of museums has a futuristic metal design which divides opinion, but one thing is clear: arguably Japan's most famous woodcutter, Katsushika Hokusai (1760–1849), had a good eye, a calm hand and a sense of humour, too. *Tue–Sun 9.30am–5.30pm | admission 400 yen | 2-7-2 Kamezawa, Sumida-ku |* 墨田区亀沢2-7-2 *| subway E 12, JR Ryogoku | hokusai-museum.jp/?lang=en |* 📖 *0*

EDO TOKYO MUSEUM (江戸東京博物館)

If you think that historical museums are a bore, think again. This spaceship-like building features replicas of the lanes of Edo, Tokyo's name in the era of the samurai. Multilingual guides show you the highlights for free (approx. 90 mins). *Tue–Fri, Sun 9.30am–5.30pm, Sat 9.30am–7.30pm | admission 600 yen | 1-4-1 Yokoami, Sumida-ku |* 墨田区横網1-4-1 *| edo-tokyo-museum.or.jp/en | subway E 12, JR Ryogoku |* 📖 *0*

UENO PARK (上野公園) 🐗

This park, with its cafés, temples and the greatest concentration of museums in the city, is always busy. During

Cute or cringe? Maid cafés in Akihabara

cherry blossom season *(hanami)*, you can picnic and celebrate here with thousands of other people. In summer, when the Shinobazu Pond on the park's south side is filled with huge lotus leaves and pink blossom, taking a picture is a must. *Daily around the clock | admission free | 5-20 Ueno-koen, Taito-ku | 台東区上野公園5-20 | subway G 16, H 17, JR Ueno |* ⚏ *e1*

YANAKA (谷中)

In *Yanaka-Ginza* in the nostalgic Yanaka quarter you can buy all kinds of sweets from street vendors. In other lanes you'll find treasures such as ceramic tea bowls and *washi* paper. The *Yanaka Cemetery*, one of Tokyo's oldest, is popular for picnics at cherry blossom time. This quarter has a large number of temples, especially on Sansaki-zaka street. In amongst the greenery is the colourful *Nezu-jinja Shrine (Sept–May daily 6am–5pm, June–Aug 5am–6pm | 1-28-9 Nezu, Bunkyo-ku | subway C 14 Nezu).* In April and May, 3,000 azaleas blossom here in all shades of white, pink and red. The orange-red gates of the Inari Fox Shrine make another great picture. ⚏ *e1*

INSIDER TIP
Abundant blossom!

AKIHABARA (秋葉原)

If you love manga, anime, cosplay and electronic gadgets, this district is heaven. On Sunday afternoons the Chuo-dori main street west of the railway station becomes a pedestrian zone. Here you'll find manga cafés as well as maid cafés, which are popular with the Otaku subculture and where young women dressed in housemaid outfits wait on guests, addressing male visitors as 'master'. The railway station area is full of electronics shops of all sizes *(e.gB. Yodobashi Camera). Subway H 15, JR Akihabara |* ⚏ *e2*

IMPERIAL PALACE (皇居)

You'll need to keep up a fast pace to follow the 5km route around the Imperial Palace. The residence covers 110,000m² and is surrounded by moats. Only the eastern garden, where the mighty Edo castle once stood, is actually accessible to tourists *(mostly Sat–Thu 9am–4pm, sometimes longer, closed 28 Dec–3 Jan | 1-1 Chiyoda, Chiyoda-ku | 千代田区千代田1-1 | kunaicho.go.jp/e-event/higashigyoen02.html | subway C 10*

Nijubashi). The gates by the Nijubashi bridge only open on 2 January and 23 February, the Emperor's birthday, when the Imperial Family waves to the crowds from the glazed balcony. At the end of March and beginning of April, the Chidorigafuchi area along the moat is a delightful mass of pink cherry blossom, illuminated at night. *d3*

INSIDER TIP *Imperial cherries*

GINZA (銀座)

Tokyo's luxury shopping mile boasts the world's big brands, but lovers of architecture will find it attractive too. Toyo Ito, for example, designed the building of the Japanese pearl brand Mikimoto and the Hermès glass cube was the brainchild of Renzo Piano. The Wako department store is known for its artistic window dressing by the Ginza crossroads. Delicious lunch boxes and premium snacks are sold in the basements of the luxury department stores *(e.g.Takashimaya).* At the weekend the main shopping mile becomes a pedestrian zone in the afternoon: great for people watching! *Subway M 16, H 08, G 09 Ginza | e4*

INSIDER TIP *Cheap delicacies*

FISH MARKET (築地市場) ★ ⚑

Nowhere on earth are more fish and seafood sold than in Tokyo's fish market. In 2018, the wholesale buildings were relocated from their long-term site at Tsukiji and placed 2km away at Toyosu. The tuna auction *(Mon–Tue, Thu–Sat, sometimes Wed | 6-6-1 Toyosu, Koto-ku |* 江東区豊洲 *6-6-1 | shijou.metro.tokyo.jp/toyosu/pdf/kenngaku/route-english.pdf | U 14, Yurikamome line Shijomae)* starts at 5.30am, but because of the large crowds you should be there at least an hour earlier.

The outer market area of *Tsukiji Jogai Shijo* (築地場外市場) remained in its original location and is therefore close enough to the Ginza shopping mile to get a sushi lunch. *Mon–Tue, Thu–Sat, sometimes Wed 7am–3pm | 4-16-2 Tsukiji, Chuo-ku |* 中央区築地4-16-2中央区築地場外市場 *| tsukiji.or.jp/english | subway H 10 Tsukiji, E 18 Tsukijishijo | f5*

HAMARIKYU ONSHI TEIEN (浜離宮恩賜庭園) ⚑

People love this 350-year-old park with the backdrop of the Shiodome skyscraper district. Surrounded by Japanese maple and pine trees, a teahouse forms the centre of the biggest pond. Here you can relax and taste the freshly brewed, green Matcha tea with seasonal sweets (sets from 510 yen). *Daily 9am–4.30pm | admission 300 yen | 1-1 Hama Rikyu-teien, Chuo-ku |* 中央区浜離宮庭園 *1-1 | teien.tokyo-park.or.jp/en/hama-rikyu/index.html | subway E 19 Shiodome | 1½ hrs | e5*

ODAIBA (お台場) 🏖

The drive to the offshore island of Odaiba is exciting in itself, and the view of the bay and the Tokyo Tower – a copy of Paris's Eiffel Tower – is superb, especially at night! In the afternoon, ferries sail between the Hamarikyu Garden and Odaiba. Alternatively, take the driverless Yurikamome transit service from Shinbashi station whose track runs on stilts and crosses the Rainbow Bridge. You won't get bored on Odaiba, a venue of the 2021 Olympics, because there are several shopping malls with restaurants and cinemas. Admire robots in the 🎦 *National Museum of Emerging Science and Innovation* (Miraikan for short) *(Wed–Mon 10am–5pm | 2-3-6 Aomi, Koto-ku | admission 620 yen, children 210 yen | miraikan.jst.go.jp/en | subway U 09 Telecom Center)* and try the latest technical gadgets in the 🐦 *Panasonic Center Tokyo (Tue–Sun 10am–6pm | admission free | 3-5-1 Ariake, Koto-ku | panasonic.com/global/corporate/center/tokyo.html | subway U 12, Yurikamome line Ariake).* The 20m tall robot statue *Unicorn Gundam* enthuses manga and anime fans who can purchase Gundam figurines and kits in the nearby *DiverCity* shopping centre. 🏛 0

MORI BUILDING DIGITAL ART MUSEUM: TEAMLAB BORDERLESS (森ビル デジタル アート ミュージアム：ームラボ ボーダレス) ★ 🎦

Immerse yourself in this huge museum in Odaiba which creates a sea of light and colour. Spectacular, digital interactive art awaits in labyrinth-like spaces with light installations in utterly bright colours. What is special here is that you become your own artist. Scanners allow you to digitise what you have painted, to change the colours via an app and integrate your piece into the overall teamLab Borderless artwork. Also great fun for children! *Mon–Fri 10am–7pm, Sat/Sun 10am–9pm, closed 2nd and 4th Tue of each month | admission 3,200 yen, children (4–14) 1,000 yen | Odaiba Palette Town, 1-3-8 Aomi, Koto-ku |* 江東区青海1-3-8お台場パレットタウン | *borderless.teamlab.art | subway U 10, Yurikamome line Aomi | book several weeks in advance at ticket.teamlab.art/#/order |* 🕐 *3 hrs |* 🏛 0

ROPPONGI (六本木)

For a long time, this area in the city centre had a reputation for catering for foreigners looking for "adventure". However, the district has changed in recent years: now you can get the best art and consumer goods here, displayed in two super-modern complexes: *Roppongi Hills (daily mostly 11am–9pm, restaurants until 11pm | 6-10-1 Roppongi, Minato-ku | subway H 04, E 23 Roppongi | roppongihills.com/en)* is identifiable by the 10-m-tall spider sculpture by Louise Bourgeois. More than 200 shops plus cinemas, restaurants and an art museum *(Mori Art Museum)* provide countless options for browsing and hanging out. The *Tokyo City View* open-air viewing platform in the *Mori Tower (Sun–Thu 10am–11pm, Fri/Sat 10am–1am | admission 1,800 yen)* offers breathtaking views of Tokyo from a height of 270m. *Roppongi Midtown* is more elegant and quieter than Roppongi Hills.

INSIDER TIP
Cool art

Do not miss the beautifully curated exhibitions in the *21_21 Design Sight*

Museum in the Midtown Garden (Wed–Mon 10am–7pm | admission 1,100 yen | 2121designsight.jp/en). ⊞ c4–5

SHIBUYA (渋谷)

Have you seen Sofia Coppola's movie *Lost in Translation*? If so, then you will remember dinosaurs on the mega-crossing, flanked by giant screens. The *Shibuya Scramble Crossing* in the popular entertainment and shopping district of Shibuya is at its busiest at the weekend and in the evening. You get a good view of the thousands of people using Shibuya railway station from the interconnecting passageway between the JR and Keio-Inokashira lines.

INSIDER TIP
Ant trail

Outside the station is a bronze statue of the dog Hachiko who waited for ten years, in exactly this spot, for his deceased master. This is now a popular meeting place. Around Shibuya railway station are many cafés, restaurants and trendy shops in huge skyscrapers – such as *Hikarie* and *Shibuya Stream*, the latter being located by the Shibuya River with its recently designed green spaces. From the outdoor viewing platform of the brand-new, 46-floor *Shibuya Scramble Square*, you cannot only see the famous crossing, but on clear days, Mount Fuji as well. ⊞ a4

HARAJUKU (原宿) & OMOTESANDO (表参道)

Fashionable teenage Tokyo, with its wacky clothes shops and cheap fast-food outlets, is situated around *Takeshita-dori* street in Harajuku; also here is one of the biggest 100-yen shops *(Daiso)*. Casual to elegant fashion for the over-30s is on sale on

Modern life: lightshow at the Shibuya Crossing

luxurious Omotesando street – Tokyo's version of the Champs-Élysées. Have a look into the side streets as well! *Subway C 04, G 02, Z 02 Omotesando |* 🕮 *a–b 4*

Meijijingumae), which serves as a communal garden for many citizens: here they picnic and have a nap; bands use it as a practice space, and Elvis fans with big hair take to the stage. 🕮 *a4*

Parisian flair along Omotesando shopping street

MEIJI SHRINE (明治神宮) & YOYOGI PARK (代々木公園)

One part of the enormous green space west of the city centre is dedicated to spirituality, the other to fun. Millions of people queue in front of the *Meiji Shrine (daily 9am–4.30pm | 2-1 Yoyogi-Kamizono-cho, Shibuya-ku |* 渋谷区代々木神園町 *2-1 | meijijingu.or.jp/english | JR Harajuku, subway C 03, F 15 Meijijingumae)* in early January to join in the first prayers of the year. The shrine is also popular for weddings. On the other side of this green oasis is the *Yoyogi Park (open around the clock | 2-1 Yoyogi-Kamizono-cho, Shibuya-ku |* 渋谷区代々木 *2-1 | JR Harajuku, subway C 03, F 15*

SHINJUKU (新宿)

The skyscraper district west of the railway station includes the 243-m-tall *Tokyo Metropolitan Building,* Tokyo's town hall. It is not pretty but imposing – and from its 45th floor you can look down onto the city for free *(daily 9.30am–11pm | admission free | 2-8-1 Nishi-Shinjuku, Shinjuku-ku | subway E 28 Tochomae).* To balance the mass of concrete, visit *Shinjuku Gyoen (Tue–Sun 9am–4pm | admission 200 yen | env.go.jp/garden/shinjukug yoen/english | subway M 10 Shinjukugyoenmae),* one of the city centre's biggest parks. When the cherry trees blossom at the end of March/early April, it is full of people, and in November it hosts a big chrysanthemum exhibition. The district also has countless shops, department stores, cafés and restaurants as well as, east of the railway station, Tokyo's biggest night-time entertainment and red-light quarter: Kabukicho. 🗺 b2–3

EATING & DRINKING

SORANOIRO NIPPON (ソラノイロ日本)

The soup is carrot-based, the noodles made from wholegrain rice, and there are fresh vegetables on top. This unassuming restaurant serves the best ramen noodle soups. As well as "normal" ramen, there are gluten-free, vegetarian and vegan varieties. *Daily 8.30am–10.30pm | Ramen Street in Tokyo railway station, B1F |* 東京駅一番街地下ラーメンストリート *B1F | subway, M 17, JR Tokyo | ¥ |* 🗺 e3

SHABUSHABU ONYASAI (しゃぶしゃぶ温野菜)

What a deal! For 25 euros per person, you can eat as much as you like for 90 minutes! Choose from several varieties of broth and order meat, vegetables and side dishes as well. The ingredients are briefly boiled in the hot soup, and then they're ready for you to dunk into a sesame dip or ponzu, a light soy-based sauce with citrus flavour. *Daily 5–11.30pm, Sat-Sun from 4pm | Yaesu YK Building 4F, 1-7-10 Yaesu, Chuo-ku |* 中央区八重洲 *1-7-10* 八重洲YKビル4F *| subway M 17, JR Tokyo | ¥ |* 🗺 e3

MANMAYA (まんまや慶応仲通り店)

This popular pub *(izakaya)* in an old wooden house in the student quarter near the Keio University is easily recognisable by the red paper screen at the entrance. Seating is on tatami rice straw mats or at wooden tables or in separate group spaces. The food is delicious! *Sat-Thu 5pm–midnight, Fri 5pm–4am | 5-20-20 Shiba, Minato-ku |* 港区芝 *5-20-20 | subway I 04, A 08 Mita, JR Tamachi | ¥ |* 🗺 d6

GONPACHI (権八 西麻布)

Just like in the movies! Hollywood director Quentin Tarantino used the Gonpachi as inspiration for some key scenes in *Kill Bill*. Here you can try a delicious cross-section of Japanese cuisine in a lively atmosphere. Perfect for a cool evening out. You better book a table online because the restaurant is hugely popular, especially with tourists! *Daily 11.30am–3.30am | 1-13-11 Nishi-Azabu, Minato-ku |* 港区西麻布 *1-13-11 | subway H 04, E 23 Roppongi | gonpachi.jp | ¥¥ |* 🗺 c5

SHOPPING

2K540 AKI OKA ARTISAN (ニーケーゴーヨンマル アキ オカ アルチザン)☂

Of course you can find beautiful arts and crafts – both traditional and with a modern touch – in all big department stores, but it is much more exciting to browse for hand-made leather, wood, lacquer and ceramics goods in this extraordinary street of shops below the Yamanote circular rail line.

Japanese tradition: the Kabukiza Theatre

bars and pubs have a mandatory evening *cover charge* (300–1,000 yen). Often you will get a small snack with your drink. You'll find nightclubs in Shibuya and Roppongi, bars with live music and cabaret in Shimokitazawa, theatre and concert halls mainly in Ginza and Shinjuku.

KABUKIZA THEATRE (歌舞伎座)

Men in female roles wearing make-up and amazing kimonos; music played on Japanese instruments; stories that combine comedy and drama – this is the ancient Japanese form of theatre known as *kabuki*. Why not buy a ticket for one act *(Hitomaku-mi)* at the box office and hire an English audio guide? *Daily at various times | admission from approx. 1,000 yen | 4-12-15 Ginza, Chuo-ku |* 中央区銀座4-12-15 *| kabuki-bito.jp/eng/top.html | subway H 09, A 11 Higashi-Ginza |* ⌑ *e4*

Thu–Tue 11am–7pm | 5-9-23 Ueno, Taito-ku | 台東区上野5-9-23 *| jrtk. jp/2k540 | subway G 14 Suehirocho, JR Okachimachi |* ⌑ *e2*

KYUKYUDO (鳩居堂)

Japan is famous for hand-made *washi* paper and in this traditional shop you will quickly see why. The paper is exquisite, decorated with ornaments and painted by hand. On the first floor you find brushes, ink stones and incense sticks. *Mon–Sat 10am–7pm, Sun 11am–7pm | 5-7-4 Ginza, Chuo-ku |* 中央区銀座5-7-4 *| subway G 09, M 16 Ginza |* ⌑ *e4*

BLUE NOTE TOKYO
(ブルーノート東京)

Candy Dulfer, Till Brönner, David Foster – jazz musicians from all over the world feel at home in this 200-seat club with an intimate and exclusive atmosphere. *Mon–Fri 5pm–midnight, Sat/Sun 3.30–11pm | admission from approx. 50 euros | Leica Bldg., 6-3-16 Minami-Aoyama, Minato-ku |* 港区南青山6-3-16ライカビル *| bluenote. co.jp | subway G 02, C 04, Z 02 Omotesando |* ⌑ *b5*

NIGHTLIFE

In Japan, going out generally means eating, drinking and karaoke. Many

SHIBUYA WOMB (渋谷ウーム)

Super electro and techno club for the weekend: great DJs on several dancefloors, exciting light and laser show. Remember to bring photo ID. *Daily approx. 11pm–5am | 2-16 Maruyama-cho, Shibuya-ku |* 渋谷区円山町 *2-16 | womb.co.jp/en | subway G 01, Z 01, F 16, JR Shibuya |* □ *a5*

WELLNESS

OEDO ONSEN MONOGATARI (大江戸温泉物語)

After a relaxing bath, put on a cotton kimono *(yukata)* and stroll through the Edo-period setting while tasting snacks from stalls as you go along. Somewhat kitsch, but truly restorative. *Daily 11am–9pm | admission Mon–Fri 2,720 yen incl. towel and yukata, from 6pm 2,180 yen, Sat–Sun 216 yen surcharge, overnight additional 2,160 yen | 2-6-3 Aomi, Minato-ku |* 江東区青海 *2-6-3 | daiba.ooedoonsen.jp/en | subway U 09 Telecom Center |* □ *0*

BEACHES

There aren't really any beaches in Tokyo, but you can surf off *Ehukai Beach* on Odaiba as well as trying out stand-up paddling and sea kayaking *(daily 10am–8pm | 3,000–8,000 yen | Marine House 1F 1-4-1 Daiba, Minato-ku | e-odaiba.com/Wind_surfing/Wind_surfing.html | subway U 06 Odaiba-Kaihinkoen |* □ *0)*. However, bathing is prohibited.

INSIDER TIP
Watersports with mega-backdrop

AROUND TOKYO

1 KAWAGOE (川越市)
50km from Tokyo / 1 hr by train

Pure nostalgia awaits you in this city (pop. 350,000), where the *Koedo* ("little Edo") quarter still has buildings from the Edo and Taisho periods, including two two-storey wooden warehouses. Try traditional sweets in Kashiyayokocho lane. You are bound to find a unique souvenir in the popular *Kawagoe Antique Market* which is held on the 28th of each month. 120 stalls provide lots of choice from odds and ends to ceramics and second-hand kimonos.

INSIDER TIP
Flea market finds

The *Kita-in Temple (15 mins from Hon-Kawagoe railway station)* was founded 1,200 years ago. Here, 540 stone statues of the Buddha from the 18th and 19th centuries are lined up, each of them carved by a different artisan. One smiles, another has a nap, while yet another appears agitated. Which one is your favourite? □ *G7*

2 NARITA-SAN SHINSHOJI TEMPLE (成田山新勝寺)
60km from Tokyo / 1½ hrs by train

In the midst of a beautiful park, one of the country's most versatile temple complexes is only a few minutes by train from Narita Airport. There are guided tours in English of the 1,000-year-old area and its temples, sutra hall and pagoda *(daily*

10am–3pm | book at naritasan_ guide@yahoo.co.jp or at the information office in front of the pagoda). Be careful not to get waylaid beforehand in Omotesando street where all kinds of things including arts and crafts and local specialities, such as grilled eel and sweet rice cakes with cherry blossom, are for sale. *Daily 9am–4pm | 1 Narita, Narita-shi, Chiba-ken |* 千葉県成田市成田1 *| naritasan.or.jp/ english | JR, Keisei Narita |* ⏱ *2 hrs |* 📖 *G7*

NIKKO NATIONAL PARK

(📖 G7) **The town of Nikko (pop. 82,000) in the north of the Kanto region, accessible from Tokyo in two hours, is the springboard to the famous sanctuaries and hiking areas in the Nikko National Park.**

If your muscles are aching, take a bath in the area's many hot springs, for example in Yumoto in the mountain region of Oku-Nikko.

SIGHTSEEING

TOSHOGU SHRINE (東照宮) & RINNOJI TEMPLE (輪王寺)

This magnificent temple precinct of 130 buildings glitters with copious amounts of lacquer and gold. It is a jewel, hidden away in the mountains and surrounded by ancient cedar forest. The entrance is via a bright red bridge across the Daiya River – the perfect photo opportunity! The decorative elements at the ★ *Toshogu Shrine* and Yomeimon Gate are unbelievably detailed and creative. Can you spot the three monkeys of Nikko? One keeps its hands over its eyes, the second over its ears and the third over its mouth. They represent the ancient Confucian saying, "hear no evil, see no evil and speak no evil".

In the recently renovated, and shiny, Rinnoji Temple you will find three towering, gold- and lacquer-coated statues of Amida in the main building. The foundation stone of the complex, which is a UNESCO World Heritage Site, was laid by a Buddhist monk in the eighth century, and most of the buildings were constructed in the 17th century. *April–Oct daily 8am–5pm, Nov–March 8am–4pm | admission 1,300 yen | 2301 Sannai, Nikko-shi, Tochigi-ken |* 栃木県日光市山内2301 *| toshogu.jp/english/index. html | 10 mins by bus from Nikk, Tobu and JR railway station or 35 mins on foot |* ⏱ *3-4 hrs*

CHUZENJI LAKE (中禅寺湖)

The picturesque lake is in the middle of dense forest whose leaves display wonderful colours at the end of October. The 100-m-tall Kegon waterfall is one of the three most beautiful in the country. *Bus (60 mins) from Nikko, Tobu and JR railway station*

AROUND TOKYO

Iiyama 飯山市
Nikko-Nationalpark
Toshogu Shrine ★
Nikkō 日光市
Hitachi 日立市
Nagano 長野市
Shibukawa 渋川市
Yuki 結城市
Saku 佐久市
Kuki 久喜市
Hokota 鉾田市
150km, 2¼ hrs
Fujimi 富士見町
Kawagoe
Narita-San-Shinshoji-Tempel
Narita 成田市
Tokio
60km, 1½ hrs
Choshi 銚子市
120km, 2½ hrs
33km, 30mins
Nirasaki 韮崎市
Yokohama
Chinatown in Yokohama ★
Fuji ★
Kamakura ★
Izu islands ★
Fuji 富士市
Fuji-Hakone-Izu National park
50 km
31.07 mi

YOKOHAMA

(*⧉ G7*) **In Japan's second largest city (pop. 3.7 million), only 30 minutes by train from Tokyo, you can feel the proximity to the sea.**

Over 160 years ago, Yokohama's extensive harbour transformed the until-then sleepy fishing village into a modern international city. Big cruise liners moor at the futuristic Osanbashi Pier.

SIGHTSEEING

YOKOHAMA LANDMARK TOWER (横浜ランドマークタワー)

In only 40 seconds the lift catapults you to the 69th floor and the viewing platform of the second tallest building in Japan. The view is particularly spectacular in the evening when the port area

INSIDER TIP
Heavenly views

and ferris wheel are illuminated! On clear days you can even see Mount Fuji. *Sun–Fri 10am–9pm, Sat 10am–10pm | admission 1,000 yen | 2-2-1 Minatomirai, Nishi-ku |* 西区み なとみらい *2-2-1 | Minato-Mirai or Sakuragicho railway station |* ⌚ *1 hr*

CUPNOODLES MUSEUM (カップ ヌードルミュージアム)

This interactive museum is dedicated to Momofuku Ando, the inventor of the instant ramen noodle soups, and here you can create your own recipe. *Wed–Mon 10am–6pm | admission 500 yen, children (up to 12) 300 yen | 2-3-4 Shinko, Naka-ku |* 中区新港

However busy it gets, nothing can disturb the inner calm of Buddha Daibutsu

2-3-4 | *cupnoodles-museum.jp/en* | *Minatomirai or Bashamichi railway station*

EATING & DRINKING

CHINATOWN (中華街) ★
The Japanese love Chinese food. You'll find particularly authentic cuisine in Japan's biggest Chinatown, with 600 shops and restaurants serving Chinese food from all regions of the Middle Kingdom. *Motomachi/Chukagai railway station*

SHOPPING

YOKOHAMA RED BRICK WAREHOUSES (横浜赤レンガ倉庫)
These brick warehouses were built more than 100 years ago, and today they house trendy small shops and a food court. The view of the Yokohama skyline is one of the most beautiful night-time scenes in Japan. *Daily 10am–7pm (building 1), 11am–8pm (building 2)* | *1-1 Shinko, Naka-ku* | 中区新港*1-1* | *yokohama-akarenga.jp/en* | *Bashamichi or Nihon-odori railway station*

KAMAKURA

(⚏ *G8)* **A great excursion leads from Tokyo in one hour to the former imperial city of ★ Kamakura (pop. 172,000) where you can admire a big Buddha, countless temples and shrines in parkland as well as beaches.**

Today, the "Kyoto of the East"

appears relaxed if not a little sleepy, but between the 12th and 14th centuries it was the political centre of Japan.

SIGHTSEEING

KITA-KAMAKURA (北鎌倉)

Start your tour through this temple complex in the *Engakuji* Zen Temple *(daily 8.30am–4.30pm | admission 300 yen | 1 min from Kitakamakura railway station, JR)*. Its Shariden hall of relics is the oldest Zen building in Japan. Continue to the *Kenchoji* Temple. Dating from 1253, it's Japan's oldest Zen monastery *(daily 8.30am–4.30pm | admission 300 yen | ⏲ 1–1½ hrs)*.

INSIDER TIP
Mythical monsters
Definitely have a look at the small *Hasonbo* Shrine at the rear which features numerous statues of the mythical creature Tengu, with long nose, beak and wings!

DAIBUTSU (大仏)

Inner peace radiates from the 13th-century seated Buddha in the Kotoku-in Temple, which is surrounded by nature. You can climb inside the 11.3m-tall and 121-tonne bronze statue for a small fee. *Daily April–Sept 8am–5.30pm, Oct–March 8am–5pm | admission 200 yen | kotoku-in.jp | Hase railway station, Enoden line | ⏲ 15 mins*

HASEDERA (長谷寺)

Close to Daibutsu is the Hasedera Temple, dedicated to Kannon, Goddess of Mercy. The multi-level area has many small statues of Jizo, in front of which believers place flowers and sweets. Jizo is the patron God of children (and their souls) who died as a result of miscarriage, stillbirth or abortion. The garden on the top level is a dream in June and July when the hydrangeas are in bloom. *Daily March–Sept 8am–5.30pm, Oct–Feb 8am–5pm | admission 300 yen | hasedera.jp/en/about | Hase railway station, Enoden line | ⏲ 1–1½ hrs*

BEACHES

The beaches of Yuigahama and Zaimokuza in Kamakura, as well as the adjacent beaches towards the Enoshima Peninsula to the west and Zushi to the east, are full of locals in July and August when lifeguards are on site. During the rest of the year, the sea belongs to the surfers who ride the waves in their hundreds – and to the foreigners. *Yuigahama railway station, Enoden line*

FUJI-HAKONE-IZU NATIONAL PARK

(*ⅢⅡ G8*) **Japan's most visited national park encompasses some key landmarks that don't necessarily belong together geographically: Japan's highest mountain Fuji-san; the five lakes that surround it; the**

Hakone region, including Ashi Lake; the Izu Peninsula, and the Izu Islands south of Tokyo.

Flora and fauna vary from mountain forest to subtropical islands. What links all of them is their volcanic character, as displayed by the conical shape of Mount Fuji.

SIGHTSEEING

ASHI LAKE (芦ノ湖) 👥

In good weather, the volcanic crater of Mount Fuji is reflected in the water of the Ashi-no-ko Lake. You get the perfect picture from a pirate-style ferry, especially if you manage to include the orange *Torii* Gate of the Hakonejinja Shrine by the shore. The journey there, on the cosy Hakone Tozan Railway to Gora and from there via cable car and ropeway, is part of the fun. *Daily mid-March–Nov 9.30am–5.30pm, Dec–mid-March 9.30am–4.40pm | ride 1,000 yen, children (up to 11) 500 yen | Togendai terminal of the Hakone ropeway*

OWAKUDANI (大涌谷)

The funny smell is due to the sulphur from the Hakone volcano's last eruption 3,000 years ago, which rises from the valley bottom. Are you brave enough to try the black eggs which have been boiled in sulphuric water? Allegedly they can prolong your life by seven years. *Owakudani terminal of the Hakone ropeway between Sounzan and Togendai*

INSIDER TIP
Egg dare

HAKONE OPEN-AIR MUSEUM
(箱根 彫刻の森美術館) 👥

You will love this outdoor museum even if you don't care much about modern art. In a garden of 70,000m², 120 over-sized sculptures are displayed, amongst them the huge Miss Black Power by Niki de Saint Phalle. *Daily 9am–5pm | admission 1,600 yen, children 800 yen | 1121 Ninotaira, Ashigarashimo-gun, Hakone-cho, Kanagawa-ken | 神奈川県足柄下郡箱根町二ノ平 1121 | hakone-oam.or.jp | Chokoku-no-Mori railway station, Hakone-Tozan line via Hakone-Yumoto railway station, Odakyu line | ⏱ 3–4 hrs*

FUJI (富士山) ★

Especially in winter, when it has a white cap of snow, the 3,776-m-high Fuji volcano radiates majestic beauty. If you are lucky, you will have already seen it from the aeroplane or from the Shinkansen bullet train to Kyoto. Japan's iconic landmark and a UNESCO World Heritage Site since 2013, Mount Fuji has inspired artists and poets and is the destination of countless pilgrims who venerate it as a deity. The Japanese call it Fuji-san. The active volcano last erupted in 1707; even Tokyo, 100km away, was covered in ash. Despite hundreds of thousands of hikers climbing Mount Fuji during the official climbing season from July to mid-September, you should never underestimate the mountain. Even if the rest of Japan suffers from a heatwave, at the top of

Mount Fuji it can be extremely cold and even snowy. A typical climbing tour takes two days. Some of the hikers sleep in chalets on the summit at above 3,000m. It is best to join a tour with experienced local guides *(e.g. fujimountainguides.com)* – but not at weekends, otherwise you may have to queue to get to the summit!

IZU ISLANDS (伊豆諸島) ★

You reach the volcanic Izu Islands south of Tokyo either by speedboat in a few hours or by overnight ferry. (The islands are not to be confused with the Izu Peninsula, from which there are also ferry connections.) The Izu Islands are wonderful for camping, hiking, fishing and bathing. ⚑ You can swim with wild dolphins in summer *(book via the touristinformationwebsite:blue@mikura-isle.com)*. An aeroplane gets you to *Hachijo-jima Island*, known for hot springs, ocean views, flying fish and a mini-version of Mount Fuji. Depending on the weather, ferries may be cancelled, so factor in some spare time. 🛥 Discounts of up to 30 per cent are available if you book early *(tokaikisen. co.jp/en/time_price/discount). Daily speedboats and ferries (tokaikisen. co.jp/en) from Takeshiba terminal, Takeshiba railway station, U 03*

INSIDER TIP
Dolphins ahead

Conquer Ashi Lake and sail past Mount Fuji in a pirate ship

CENTRAL JAPAN

CULTURAL RICHES – PAST & PRESENT

For a long time, the Kansai region in central Japan was the cultural and political heart of the country. Kyoto and Nara, both some-time imperial residences, are famous throughout the world for their historical heritage.

Compared to the dynamic capital of Tokyo, people in central Japan enjoy a slower pace of life, although this is increasingly difficult given the number of visitors to Kyoto. Traditionally a city of merchants, Osaka is the second-most important economic centre after

The Kinkaku-ji in Kyoto is known as the "Golden Temple" for a reason

Tokyo. The archetype of the streetwise trader lives on among the city's residents, who are known for their vitality, strong accents and sense of humour.

Together with the port city of Kobe, Osaka and Kyoto form one of the world's biggest metropolitan regions, home to more than 24 million people. But the region is also rural in many parts, with the surrounding prefectures of Fukui, Shiga or Wakayama characterised by rice fields, mountains and forests.

CENTRAL JAPAN

Wajima 輪島市

Nanao 七尾市

Shika 志賀町

Hakui 羽咋市

Himi 氷見市

Tsubata 津幡町

Toyama 富山市

Hakusan 白山市

Kanazawa ★ p.84

Komatsu 小松市

Shirakawa-go 41

8

Fukui Prefectural Dinosaur Museum

Takayama p.87

7

Fukui 福井市

Ono 大野市

Echizen 越前市

Gero 下呂市

Ikeda 池田町

Tsuruga 敦賀市

Gujo 郡上市

Kyotango 京丹後市

Ine 伊根町

Nagahama 長浜市

12 Kinosaki Onsen

Maizuru 舞鶴市

Obama 小浜市

Gifu 岐阜市

27

Yabu 養父市

Hikone 彦根市

Nagoya p.87

Toyota 9

145km, 2 hrs 20mins

Tamba 丹波市

Fushimi Inari-Taisha ★

Kuwana 桑名市

Sasayama 篠山市

11 Enryaku-ji

130km, 44mins

Kyoto p.88

Koka 甲賀市

Handa 半田市

30km, 12mins

Kaiyukan Aquarium ★

Suzuka 鈴鹿市

14 Himeji Castle ★

Todai-ji ★

Osaka p.94

Nara p.93

Awaji 淡路市

28

Kobe p.98

Ise 伊勢市

Sakai 堺市

Kashihara 橿原市

10 Ise-jingu ★

Sumoto 洲本市

Wakayama 和歌山市

13 Koya-san ★

Taiki 大紀町

Shima 志摩市

42

Aridagawa 有田川町

Owase 尾鷲市

Yura 由良町

Inami 印南町

Anan 阿南市

42

Sea of Japan

PACIFIC OCEAN

Kiho 紀宝町

Susami すさみ町

Nachi-Katsuura 那智勝浦町

50 km
31.06 mi

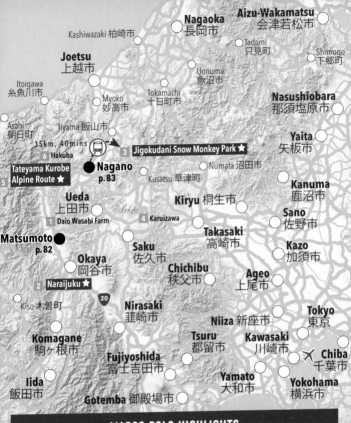

Kashiwazaki 柏崎市

Nagaoka 長岡市

Aizu-Wakamatsu 会津若松市

Tadami 只見町

Shimogo 下郷町

Joetsu 上越市

Uonuma 魚沼市

Nasushiobara 那須塩原市

Itoigawa 糸魚川市

Myoko 妙高市

Tokamachi 十日町市

Asahi 朝日町

Iiyama 飯山市

Yaita 矢板市

35km, 40mins

3 Jigokudani Snow Monkey Park ★

Hakuba

Nagano p. 83

Kanuma 鹿沼市

Tateyama Kurobe Alpine Route ★

5

Kusatsu 草津町

Numata 沼田市

Sano 佐野市

Ueda 上田市

Kiryu 桐生市

1 Daio Wasabi Farm

4 Karuizawa

Kazo 加須市

Matsumoto p. 82

Saku 佐久市

Takasaki 高崎市

Okaya 岡谷市

Chichibu 秩父市

Ageo 上尾市

Kiso 木曽町

2 **Naraijuku ★**

20

Nirasaki 韮崎市

Niiza 新座市

Tokyo 東京

Komagane 駒ヶ根市

Tsuru 都留市

Kawasaki 川崎市

Chiba 千葉市

Fujiyoshida 富士吉田市

Yamato 大和市

Iida 飯田市

Gotemba 御殿場市

Yokohama 横浜市

MARCO POLO HIGHLIGHTS

★ **NARAIJUKU**
Time-travel to "old Japan" in this former Edo-period staging post between Kyoto and Tokyo ➤ p. 83

★ **JIGOKUDANI SNOW MONKEY PARK**
Watch Japan's monkeys taking a hot bath in winter ➤ p. 83

★ **TATEYAMA KUROBE ALPINE ROUTE**
Buses and cars look like toys next to the 20-m-high walls of snow ➤ p. 84

★ **KANAZAWA**
Visit teahouses in the traditional geisha districts ➤ p. 84

★ **ISE-JINGU**
Feel the power of one of Japan's holiest sites ➤ p. 88

★ **FUSHIMI INARI-TAISHA**
Thousands of gates line the winding path to this shrine – a unique sight south of Kyoto ➤ p. 90

★ **TODAI-JI**
In the old imperial city of Nara, a colossal Buddha sits in one of the world's largest wooden buildings ➤ p. 94

★ **KAIYUKAN AQUARIUM**
Whale sharks, rays, jellyfish – breathtaking underwater worlds in Osaka ➤ p. 96

★ **KOYA-SAN**
Experience the world of Buddhist monks up close ➤ p. 98

★ **HIMEJI CASTLE**
Japan's most beautiful castle looks fantastic thanks to recent renovation work ➤ p. 99

MATSUMOTO

(▢ F7) **The second largest city (pop. 240,000) in Nagano Prefecture is famous for its imposing castle, which has the oldest keep in the country.**

Don't miss Nakamachi-dori street in the old merchants' quarter, 10 minutes on foot from the castle. Here you can find traditional sweets, artisan workshops and sophisticated restaurants. The city is compact and an ideal jumping-off point for excursions to the surrounding countryside.

SIGHTSEEING

MATSUMOTO CASTLE (松本城)

When the pink cherry blossom comes out in spring, the 16th/17th-century castle makes for a great picture, although the black fortress with its red

bridge across the moat is a magnificent sight at other times of the year as well. The top floor is accessible via narrow, steep wooden stairs. You have to climb in your socks as shoes are not allowed! *Daily 8.30am–5pm | admission 610 yen | 4-1 Marunouchi, Matsumoto-shi, Nagano-ken |* 長野県松本市丸の内*4-1 | matsumoto-castle.jp/lang | Matsumotojo-Shiyakushomae bus station |* ⏱ *1 hr*

AROUND MATSUMOTO

◼ DAIO WASABI FARM (大王わさび農場)

14km from Matsumoto / 45–60 mins by train and bus

On this farm you will learn all about *wasabi*, or Japanese horseradish,

Forget chilli: try finely ground wasabi at Daio Wasabi Farm

INSIDER TIP
Wasabi for the brave

which adds piquancy to sushi and other dishes. Try wasabi ice cream, wasabi chocolate or wasabi beer. Film fans will also love this place: they will recognise the waterwheels from Akira Kurosawa's film *Dreams* (1989). *March–Oct daily 9am–5.20pm, Nov–Feb 9am–4.30pm | admission free | 3640 Hotaka, Azumino-shi, Nagano-ken |* 長野県安曇野市穂高3640 *| Hotaka railway station, JR, then by shuttle bus (500 yen) | ⊞ F7*

☑ NARAIJUKU (奈良井宿) ★ ▏

40km from Matsumoto / 40 mins by train

Stroll past traditional houses, sit in cafés and explore the many arts and crafts shops selling locally made lacquerware. The village of Naraijuku is one of the best-preserved staging posts along the old Nakasendo road in the Kiso Valley, which was used to transport mail between Kyoto and Tokyo during the Edo period. Stay overnight in family B&Bs. *Naraijuku railway station, JR | ⊞ F7*

NAGANO

(⊞ F7) **This city (pop. 376,000), surrounded by mountains, hosted the Winter Olympics in 1998, and you can visit some of the venues. The climate is cool in summer and snowy in winter. Accordingly, you will find dozens of ski regions around Nagano.**

SIGHTSEEING

SHINSHU ZENKO-JI (信州善光寺)

The people of Nagano have been praying at this Buddhist temple for 1,400 years. There is a magical atmosphere in winter when the complex is covered in snow. At weekends, a group of volunteers, *Bonsho no Kai (book at bonshonokai@yahoo.co.jp)*, offers free guided tours in English. If you get up early, you can join the morning service

INSIDER TIP
Greet the sun in Japanese

(O-Asaji) at sunrise. *Daily approx. 6am–4pm depending on the season | 491 Motozen-machi, Nagano-shi, Nagano-ken |* 長野県長野市元善町491 *| zenkoji.jp/ENGLISH/about/index.html | Zenkoji-Daimon bus station*

AROUND NAGANO

☑ JIGOKUDANI SNOW MONKEY PARK (地獄谷野猿公苑) ★ ☺

35km from Nagano / 40 mins by bus
Japanese macaques love to bathe in hot springs in winter, and they don't seem to be disturbed by the tourists who come to this narrow river valley to watch them. Before you visit, check via webcam *(en.jigokudani-yaenkoen.co.jp/livecam2/video.html)* whether there are any monkeys on site. Best times are January and February. If you would like to dip into the hot water

yourself, the valley is close to popular towns with hot springs, such as Shibu Onsen and Yudanaka Onsen. *April–Oct daily 8.30am–5pm, Nov–March 9am–4pm | admission adults 800 yen, children 400 yen | 6845 Hirao, Yamanouchi-machi, Shimotakai-gun, Nagano-ken |* 長野県下高井郡山ノ内町大字平穏*6845 | en. jigokudani yaenkoen.co.jp. | Snow Monkey Park bus station (4–10 buses daily from Nagano, tickets 1,400 yen) |* ▢ *G7*

4 KARUIZAWA (軽井沢市)
75km from Nagano /1¾ hrs by train
When it gets too hot in Tokyo, people like to escape to the cooler resort town of Karuizawa (pop. 19,000). At an altitude of 1,000m at the base of the active Asama volcano, Karuizawa is popular with cyclists, golfers and hikers, especially when the leaves show wonderful autumn colours between mid-October and early November. The small town has a European feel, with countless boutiques, cafés and shops selling arts, crafts and local specialities, as well as a giant outlet mall *(Prince Shopping Plaza). Karuizawa railway station |* ▢ *G7*

5 TATEYAMA KUROBE ALPINE ROUTE (立山黒部アルペンルート) ★
75km from Nagano / 3 hrs by bus to the snow walls
The mountains of Niigata have the highest snowfall in the world with up to 30m or 40m annually! Next to the gigantic walls of snow, even coaches look like toys *(alpen-route.com/en).* Getting there is part of the adventure

(schedule a whole day), and involves bus, trolley bus, ropeway and cable car, and foot via the Kurobe dam. You can hike there in summer and autumn. *Bus No. 25 from Nagano railway station (eastern entrance) to Omachi (60 mins), several stops to Ogizawa, from there to the snow walls (1¾ hrs, 2,600 yen, approx. mid-April–Nov) |* ▢ *F7*

6 HAKUBA (白馬村)
44km from Nagano / 1 hr and 10 mins by bus
This large village (pop. 9,000) in the Northern Alps is in one of the best winter sports regions in Japan *(hakubavalley.com/en/ski_resort_ info)* with nine ski resorts. Around 10m of snow annually are perfect for all kinds of winter sports, even snowmobile and heli-skiing. Après-ski and nightlife are also on hand. From June to October you can join organised hiking tours. *Alpico bus to Hakuba every half hour to hour (tickets 1,800 yen) from Nagano railway station |* ▢ *F7*

KANAZAWA

(▢ *F7*) **The castle city of** ★ **Kanazawa (pop. 465,000) has largely preserved its traditional architecture.**

During the Edo period, the capital of the Ishikawa Prefecture was the seat of the wealthy Maeda clan, the second-most powerful feudal lords in the country. This is still in evidence today in the rich cultural heritage, comparable to that of Kyoto and Tokyo.

The Kenroku-en is among the three most beautiful gardens in Japan

SIGHTSEEING

NAGAMACHI SAMURAI QUARTER (長町)

Walking through the lanes between the walled residences of the samurai is like time-travelling. Despite the admission fee, it is worth visiting the *Nomura-ke samurai residence (April–Sept daily 8.30am–5.30pm, Oct–March 8.30am–4.30pm | admission 550 yen | 1-3-32 Nagamachi, Kanazawa-shi, Ishikawa-ken | 石川県金沢市長町 1-3-32 | Korinbo bus station)*. It dates from 1843 and has a small but stunning Zen garden.

KENROKU-EN (兼六園)

This landscaped garden, one of the three most beautiful in the country, is lovely at all times of the year. The extensive park was once the outer garden of *Kanazawa Castle (opening times same as Kenroku-en | admission may be chargeable)* directly opposite. From a hill you get superb views of the numerous maple, cherry and plum trees, plus beds of irises and azalea shrubs, while benches around the big man-made pond in the centre invite you to rest. The garden is also known for the skilfully placed conical ropes which protect the conifers from snow damage in winter. *March–15 Oct daily 7am–6pm, 16 Oct–Feb 8am–5pm, early opening April–Aug 4am–7am, Nov 6am–8am | admission 310 yen, I early opening free | 1-4 Kenrokumachi, Kanazawa-shi, Ishikawa-ken | 石川県金沢市兼六町 1-4 | pref.ishikawa. jp/siro-niwa/kenrokuen/e | Kenrokuen bus station, Kanazawa loop bus (LL 9, RL 8)*

CHAYAGAI TEA HOUSE QUARTER
(茶屋街)

Kanazawa has three well-preserved tea house quarters: Higashichayagai, Nishichayagai and Kazue-machichayagai. In the tea houses *(chaya)*, geishas dance and sing for guests. In Higashichayagai, two tea houses are accessible to tourists: the *Shima Tea House (daily 9am–6pm | admission 500 yen)* is a geisha museum whereas tea is actually served in the *Kaikaro Tea House (daily 9am–5pm | admission 750 yen incl. tea)*. The other buildings, all of which have two floors and are clad with wood, house cafés and shops selling local specialities and arts and crafts. *10 mins by Kanazawa loop bus from Kanazawa railway station, Hashibacho (Koban-mae) bus station, RL5*

Tea houses also have dance and music performances

EATING & DRINKING

HYAKUYAKU (百薬)

"Freestyle" is the owner's jolly answer to the question whether his cuisine is vegan or vegetarian. The lunchtime menu with tofu and vegetables is delicious and healthy. Dishes can be altered to accommodate dietary requirements, including allergies. *Tue–Fri 11am–3pm, Sat–Mon 5.30–8.30pm | 2-3-23-2 Nagamachi | 長町 2-3-23-2 | ¥*

> INSIDER TIP
> **A tailored lunch**

SHOPPING

HAKUZA (箔座)

Everything in this shop in the Higashichayagai tea house quarter is made of gold leaf, even face creams and golden facial oil blotting paper *(aburatori)*. *Daily 9.30am–6pm, in winter 9.30am–5.30pm | 10 mins by Kanazawa loop bus from Kanazawa railway station, Hashibacho (Koban-mae) bus station, RL5*

AROUND KANAZAWA

⑦ FUKUI PREFECTURAL DINOSAUR MUSEUM
(福井県立恐竜博物館) 🦖
70km from Kanazawa / 1 hr and 40 mins by car

This huge outdoor museum has 42 complete skeletons, many of which are of rare Asian dinosaurs. You can hunt for fossils yourself on a guided tour (book online). *Daily 9am–5pm, except 2nd/4th Wed of each month | admission 720 yen, students 410 yen, primary school children 260 yen | 51-11 Murokocho Terao, Katsuyama-shi, Fukui-ken |* 福井県勝山市村岡町寺尾 *51-11 | dinosaur.pref.fukui.jp/en | 10 mins by taxi from Katsuyama railway station |* ⏱ *4 hrs |* 🗺 *F7*

TAKAYAMA

(🗺 F7) **Because of its well-preserved old town with Edo-period houses, Takayama (pop. 88,000) is also called "Little Kyoto".**

Best the best times to visit are during festivals in April and October when gigantic floats parade through the streets. Try the deliciously tender Hida beef.

SIGHTSEEING

HIDA FOLK VILLAGE (飛騨の里)
In the museum village on the edge of town you learn about life in the mountains during the Edo period. Opposite, in the *Hida Takayama Crafts Experience Center (15–60 mins | from 600 yen | no booking required)* you can get creative at various workshops. *Daily 8.30am–5pm | admission 700 yen | 1-590 Kamioka-motomachi, Takayama-shi, Gifu-ken |* 岐阜県高山市上岡本町 *1-590 | hidanosato-tpo.jp/english12.htm | 10 mins by bus from Takayama railway station, Hida-no-sato bus station |* ⏱ *1½ hrs*

AROUND TAKAYAMA

8 SHIRAKAWA-GO (白川郷) 🚩
45km from Takayama / 53 mins by bus
Deep in forested mountains is the village of Shirakawa-go (pop. 1,600), a UNESCO World Heritage Site that is famous for its farmhouses which have steep roofs that look like hands folded for prayer. Since the 17th century, the tall attics have been used to keep silkworms and make gunpowder. Best travel times are May or August to October. You can stay in family-owned B&Bs in the village *(ml.shirakawa-go.org/en/accommodation)* and bathe in local hot springs. 🗺 *F7*

NAGOYA

(🗺 F8) **Nagoya (pop. 2.3 million) is a modern business city between Tokyo and Kyoto. Around the railway station are elegant skyscrapers with chic shopping malls such as** *Midland Square* **or** *JR Central Towers.*

Japan's fourth largest city is a practical starting point for excursions to the region. It is known for culinary delights such as the *kishimen* and *misonikomi-udon* noodle dishes as well as a red soy bean paste *(miso)*, which is served with *(misokatsu)*, the Japanese version of a cutlet.

SIGHTSEEING

NAGOYA CASTLE (名古屋城)

Since its construction in the 16th century, the castle has been destroyed and rebuilt several times. The 17th century *Honmaru Palace*, regarded as one of the most beautiful in Japan, burned to the ground in World War II, but thankfully many of its movable walls and murals could be saved. The ongoing reconstruction program using traditional building methods started in 2009. *Daily 9am–4.30pm | admission 500 yen, free English tour around 1pm | Nagoyajo Seimon-Mae bus station | ⏱ 1½–2 hrs*

AROUND NAGOYA

⑨ TOYOTA (豊田市)
38km from Nagoya / 1 hr and 10 mins by train

Until 1959, the city (426,000) was called Koromo, before being renamed in honour of the region's biggest employer: the Toyota car manufacturer. A 🐦 *free factory tour (Mon–Fri 11am–1pm)* shows you their production lines close by. You will need to book online weeks in advance *(toyota. co.jp/service/planttour/reservation/ ?lng=en)*. In the 🐦 *Toyota Kaikan Museum (daily 9.30am–5pm | admission free | 1 Toyota-cho, Toyota-shi, Aichi-ken | toyota.co.jp/en/about_ toyota/facility/toyota_kaikan | 20 mins on foot from Miwaka-Toyota railway*

station) you can sit in the latest models. 📖 *F8*

⑩ ISE-JINGU (伊勢神宮) ★
38km from Nagoya / 1 hr and 10 mins by train

Japan's holiest Shinto shrine is dedicated to the Sun Goddess Amaterasu. Her symbol, a mirror, is kept in the inner *Naiku Shrine* while a protective deity resides in the outer *Geku Shrine*. The building has a simple design: straightforward wooden structures with straight roofs, surrounded by fences and gravel paths. The shrine, which is regarded as a sacred site and power spot, is demolished and rebuilt every 20 years, with the 63rd rebuild scheduled for 2033. The shopping and restaurant mile of *Oharai-machi (Jan–April and Sept daily 5am–6pm, May–Aug 5am–7pm, Oct–Dec 5am–5pm | 52 Uji Imazaike-cho, Ise-shi, Mie-ken | 三重県伊勢市宇治今在家町 52 | Jingukaikan-mae bus station)* at the entrance to the Naiku Shrine is worth visiting. *Oct–Dec daily 5am–5pm, Jan–April and Sept 5am–6pm, May–Aug 5am–7pm | admission free | bus from Ise-shi railway station |* 📖 *F8*

KYOTO

(📖 E8) **Kyoto (pop. 1.47 million) presents itself as a curious mixture of the old, the surprisingly dull and the futuristically modern, such as the railway station, designed by Hiroshi Hara.**

As fine as a spider's web: the steel roof of Kyoto's enormous railway station

From 794 to 1868, the Japanese Emperor resided in Kyoto – hence the incredible cultural wealth of the city. This is probably why the Americans spared the city from bombing in World War II. Kyoto ranks highly on the must-see list for tourists, especially during cherry blossom time and for the autumnal leaves, when all major attractions are overrun by visitors. During these seasons it is advisable to visit the lesser-known temples, shrines and gardens instead.

SIGHTSEEING

HEIAN-JINGU (平安神宮)

The bright orange of this shrine from 1895 impressively contrasts with the green of the curved roofs. A 24-m-tall *torii* gate points the way. A walk in the garden with several interconnected ponds is lovely. Do you remember Charlotte, the protagonist of the cult movie *Lost in Translation*, crossing a pond on round stepping stones? Try it yourself! *Daily 6am–6pm | temple admission free, garden 600 yen | 97 Okazaki-*

INSIDER TIP
Jump across the pond

WHERE TO START?

Catch a bus from the railway station to the *Kiyomizu-dera Temple* on the hills in the eastern part of the city. There are wonderful views of Kyoto from the wooden terrace and intriguing narrow lanes to explore in the area around the temple.

Nishi-tenno-cho, Sakyo-ku | 左京区
岡崎西天王町97 | Okazakikoen-
Bijutsukan-Heian-Jingu-mae bus
station | ⏱ 1½ hrs

KIYOMIZU-DERA (清水寺)

The views of Kyoto from the imposing wooden veranda in front of the main hall are worth a visit in themselves! Admittedly, other less-crowded temples are more suitable if you are looking for a meditative experience. The 13-m-high veranda has even become a Japanese saying: when faced with a challenge, people say that they're "jumping off the stage at Kiyomizu-dera", a bit like saying "taking the plunge" in English. The small *Jishu-jinja* Shrine behind it is easily overlooked.

INSIDER TIP
Love challenge

In its grounds are two "lucky stones": if you can manage to walk the 10-m distance from one stone to the other with your eyes closed, you will be lucky in love. Likewise, taking a few sips from the three springs by the *Otowa* waterfall guarantees a healthy and successful life. And take a selfie in front of Japan's tallest three-level pagoda. *Daily 6am–6pm, sometimes open in the evening | admission 300 yen | 1-294 Kiyomizu, Higashiyama-ku |* 東 山区清水1-294 | *10 mins of foot from Gojozaka bus station |* ⏱ 2 hrs

SANJUSANGEN-DO (三十三間堂) ☔

Your head may start spinning from all the heads, arms and goddesses, but it isn't an optical illusion: 1,001 life-size statues of Bodhisattva Kannon, the Goddess of Mercy, are lined up in this 120-m long temple hall. Each of the statues, carved from cypress wood in the 12th and 13th centuries and decorated with gold leaf, has 11 heads and – symbolically – 1,000 arms to assist people in their battle with suffering. You will actually count just 42 arms per goddess, but that's still impressive! *April–15 Nov daily 8am–5pm, 16 Nov–March 9am–4pm | admission 600 yen | 657 Sanjusangendo-mawari-cho, Higashiyama-ku |* 東山区三十三間 堂廻町657 | *Hakubutsukan-sanjusangendo-mae bus station*

FUSHIMI INARI-TAISHA (伏見稲荷大社) ★

Hiking and culture are on offer at this unique shrine, dedicated to the Inari rice deities. Foxes are their protectors, which is why you will find fox statues and votive boards with their image here. A trail with hundreds of orange wooden gates winds 233m uphill through the forest to the peak of Mount Inari *(2–3 hrs return hike)*. It is best to get up early to avoid the many tourists later in the day. *Daily around the clock | admission free | 68 Fukakusa Yabunouchicho, Fushimi |* 伏見区深 草藪之内町68 | *JR station Inari |* ⏱ 2 hrs

KINKAKU-JI (金閣寺)

The Golden Pavilion is another must – and another crowded location. Luckily, pine-lined paths guide you around the pavilion so that you can take great pictures despite the many visitors, e.g.

KYOTO

Kinkaku-ji

Sarasa Nishijin Sento Cafe

Imadegawa dori

今出川通

Kawaramachi dori

Nishioji-dori

Horikawa-dori

Higashioji dori

Shirakawa dori 白川通; 京都市道182号銀上高野線

Marutamachi-dori

丸太町通

Heian-jingu

東大路通

下鴨本通

Arashiyama bamboo forest

Oike-dori 御池通

Sanjo Street

Nishiki Ichiba market

西大路通; 京都市道181号京都環状線

Shijo-dori 四条通; 京都市道186号嵐山祇園線

堀川通

Kiyomizu-dera

Shichijo-dori

Omiya-dori

Wakuden

Sanjusangen-do

Jujo-dori St. 十条通り

Fushimi Inari-Taisha ★

1 km
0.62 mi

of the reflection of the gold-leaf decorated temple in the pond. *Daily 9am–5pm | admission 400 yen | 1 Kinkakujicho, Kita-ku |* 北区金閣寺町1 *| Kinkakuji-mae bus station |* ⏱ *45 mins*

ARASHIYAMA BAMBOO FOREST
(竹林の小径)

A 400-m-long trail leads through the Arashiyama bamboo forest, one of the most popular photo locations in Kyoto – and therefore often overcrowded. *Daily around the clock | admission free | Arashiyama, Ukyo-ku |* 右京区嵐山 *| JR station Saga-Arashiyama*

Only muscle power and teamwork get the floats moving at the Gion Matsuri

EATING & DRINKING

WAKUDEN

Be here before 11am because the first dozen guests get premium Kyoto cuisine for only 2,700 yen. The creative and delicious *kaiseki* dishes with regional ingredients are worth it! *Daily 11am–3pm, 5–10pm | 11F JR Kyoto Isetan, Higashi Shiokoji-cho, Shiokoji-sagaru, Karasuma-dori, Shimogyo-ku* | 下京区烏丸通塩小路下ル東塩小路町 | *wakuden.jp/en/ryotei/kyoto* | ¥¥

SARASA NISHIJIN SENTO CAFE (さらさ西陣)

This former bathhouse with original rose-patterned tiles serves a mixture of Japanese and Western as well as vegan dishes. *Thu–Tue noon–11pm | 11-1 Murasakino Higashifujinomoricho, Kitaku* | 京都市北区紫野東藤ノ森町 11-1 | *Daitoku-ji-mae bus station* | ¥

SHOPPING

NISHIKI-ICHIBA MARKET (錦市場)

Known as "Kyoto's kitchen", more than 130 stalls, shops and restaurants are side by side underneath a covered street. Many of them have been run by the same family for generations. Try fish, meat, dried food, tofu, vegetables, pickled food, cookware and knives. *Daily 9am–5pm depending on the shop* | *Nishikikoji-dori, between Teramachi and Takakura, Nakagyo-ku* | 中京区錦小路通寺町～高倉間 | *Shijo railway station*

SPORT & ACTIVITIES

HOZUGAWA-KUDARI

This 16-km-long whitewater tour on the Hozugawa River is an unforgettable experience. The skippers steer the long

INSIDER TIP
Adrenaline rush

boats extremely close to the rocks and through rapids. *Daily 9am–5pm | tickets (2 hrs) 4,100 yen, children (4–12) 2,700 yen | hozugawakudari.jp/en | Torokko Romantic Train from Torokko Saga railway station next to Arashiyama railway station to Kameoka in 25 mins*

FESTIVALS

GION MATSURI (祇園祭)

The highlight of the famous festivals, which have been held annually on 17th and 24th July since the ninth century, are the magnificent parades of floats, some up to 25m tall, around the *Yasaka-jinja Shrine (daily around the clock | admission free | 625 Kitagawa, Gion-machi, Higashiyama-ku | 東山区祇園町北側625 | Gion bus station | ⏱ 30 mins).*

4pm, Jan–Feb 9am–4.30pm in the Todo area, Saito and Yokawa open 30 mins later and close 30 mins earlier | admission 700 yen (entire complex), 500 yen (treasury) | 4220 Sakamoto Honmachi, Otsu-shi, Shiga-ken | 滋賀県大津市坂本本町4220 | Sakamoto cable car from Hieizan-Sakamoto railway station | ⏱ 4 hrs | ▥ E8*

🖭 KINOSAKI ONSEN (城崎温泉)
145km from Kyoto / 2 hrs and 20 mins by train

Kinosaki by the Sea of Japan has been a popular spa for centuries, thanks to its hot springs. Stay in a traditional *ryokan* hostels and stroll in your *yukata* (cotton kimono) and wooden sandals along a willow-lined stream from one bath to another. *Kinosaki Onsen railway station | ▥ E7*

AROUND KYOTO

🖭 ENRYAKU-JI (延暦寺)
15km from Kyoto / 1 hr and 10 mins by train

Especially on rainy days, this temple complex in a cedar forest, a UNESCO World Heritage Site, has a mystical quality. In times past, 3,000 buildings – home to thousands of monks – stood on Mount Hieizan north-east of Kyoto. Today only a small part remains, but the importance of the 788 CE monastery as one of Japan's key spiritual centres is still tangible today. *March–Nov daily 8.30am–4.30pm, Dec 9am–*

NARA

(▥ E8) **This compact city (pop. 356,000) features gardens, temples, shrines and original residences in Edo-period style, plus more than a thousand wild and free-range deer. Nara is one of the most beautiful destinations in central Japan.**

Nara, 1,300 years ago, was the first Japanese capital and an imperial city. Deer have been revered as sacred for centuries and hunting them is prohibited. Tame and trusting, they can cause traffic chaos. If you are snacking, watch out that a deer doesn't snatch it!

INSIDER TIP
Beware of bambi

SIGHTSEEING

TODAI-JI (東大寺) ★

The path through the impressive dark wooden gate from the Kamakura period is awesome: gigantic, grim-looking, protective Nio deities stare at you from both sides. Founded in 752 as the Buddhist mother temple in Japan, the Todai-ji's main hall is one the world's largest wooden buildings. Inside, you'll find a 15m-tall bronze statue of the Buddha on a lotus flower. There is also a column with a hole at floor level whose size

INSIDER TIP
Buddha's nostril

is said to correspond to the nostril of the big Buddha. If you can squeeze yourself through this opening, you are guaranteed enlightenment – in the next life! *April–Oct daily 7.30am–5.30pm, Nov–March 8am–5pm | admission 600 yen | 406-1 Zoushi-cho | 雑司町 406-1 | todaiji.or.jp/english | Daibutsuden Kasuga-Taisha-Mae bus station |* ⏱ *45 mins*

KASUGA TAISHA (春日大社)

This fascinating shrine is famous for its countless bronze lanterns in many shapes which were donated by pilgrims. The access path through a wood is flanked by large stone lanterns. *Outer area April–Sept daily 6am–6pm, Oct–March 6.30am–5pm, inner area daily 8.30am–4pm | outer area admission free, inner area 500 yen | kasugataisha.or.jp/about/index_en.html | Kasuga Taisha-Honden bus station |* ⏱ *1½–2½ hrs*

EATING & DRINKING

IMANISHI (HARUSHIKA) SAKE BREWERY
(今西清兵衛商店・春鹿)

Harushika sake tastes dry and slightly floral. Try for yourself at this brewery from 1884 in the Naramachi quarter. Nara is regarded as the birthplace of rice wine in Japan – thousands of years ago! *Daily 9am–5pm | tasting 500 yen | 24-1 Fukuchiincho | 福智院町 24-1 | 20 mins on foot from JR station Nara*

OSAKA

(▨ E8) **Japan's third largest city (pop. 2.7 million) has always competed with Tokyo.**

Since the early Edo period, Osaka has been a port city, characterised by cosmopolitan merchants. Here, people love to do business and to celebrate success. They may seem more straightforward and more welcoming than their compatriots in Tokyo. And how do you know instantly that you are in

---

WHERE TO START?

Immerse yourself in the labyrinth-like shopping district of *Dotonbori*, with its captivating lights, colours and sounds. Then taste the hearty local cuisine in a pub and, in the evening, visit a karaoke venue or a club for the perfect Osaka experience.

Osaka and not in Tokyo? On the escalator you stand on the right instead of the left – another result of the city's contact with the outside world.

SIGHTSEEING

OSAKA CASTLE (大阪城)

The current building was constructed in 1931 from reinforced concrete and is prettier outside than inside. A wide moat surrounds the large park. Founded in the 16th century, it was once the largest castle in the country, but it only managed to deter invaders for a few decades. *Daily 9am–5pm | admission 600 yen | 1-1 Osakajo, Chuo-ku |* 中央区大阪城 *1-1 | osak-acastle.net/english | JR station Osakajo-koen |* ⏱ *45 mins*

DOTONBORI (道頓堀)

You are swimming in a sea of colourful neon lights and billboards by a canal. In between are countless restaurants and shops – this is Osaka's popular entertainment district at the Ebisubashi bridge. Here you will also find Osaka's symbols on the facades: a huge red crab and the running Glico man, an LED advertising board for sweets. *Namba railway station*

UMEDA SKY BUILDING
(梅田スカイビル) 🎎

The doughnut-shaped viewing platform of the Kuchu Teien Observatory on the 39th and 40th floors of this skyscraper has a space-age feel. The towers are connected by escalators high up in the air. The platform offers a phenomenal 360-degree view of Osaka that is especially breathtaking at sunset. Feel the wind on your skin on the open-air terrace 170m above the ground. *Daily 9.30am– 10.30pm | admission 1,500 yen,*

> INSIDER TIP
> **Sunset views**

Shrill, glittery and neon-lit: Osaka's popular Dotonbori entertainment quarter

children (5–12) 700 yen | 1-1-88 Oyodonaka, Kita-ku | 北区大淀中 1-1-88 | kuchu-teien.com/en | JR station Osaka | ⏱ 1 hr

EATING & DRINKING

AJINOYA (味乃家) 🚩
Have you tried pancakes à la Japan? Okonomiyaki, a specialty of Osaka, are thick pancakes, fried on a hotplate and served with sauces and bonito flakes. We recommend the mixed version with pork, shrimps, octopus, minced meat and cabbage. Tue–Fri noon–11pm, Sat/Sun 11.30am–11pm | 1-7-16 Namba, Chuo-ku | 中央区難波 1-7-13 | Namba railway station | ¥

STREAMER COFFEE COMPANY SHINSAIBASHI (ストリーマー コーヒーカンパニー 心斎橋店)
A "military latte"? What's that? Green tea with a shot or, to be more precise, matcha latte with espresso. The owner of the cool café chain is world champion in the "art of latte", i.e. the art of creating images in the coffee foam. Trendy loft style, with skateboards on the walls. Daily 9am–9pm | 1-10-19 Nishishinsaibashi, Chuo-ku | 中央区西心斎橋 1-10-19 | Shinsaibashi railway station | ¥¥

SHOPPING

If you love shopping, Osaka is a paradise of shops and malls. At the Osaka railway station alone, you can get lost in several underground shopping streets, and the same applies to Namba railway station. Above ground and covered is the longest shopping street in Japan: Tenshinbashisuji-Shotengai (Ogimachi railway station) with more than 600 shops. More traditional is the Kuromon Ichiba Market (daily approx. 9am–6pm depending on the shop | 2-4-1 Nihombashi, Chuo-ku | Nipponbashi subway station). Here, locals and restaurant chefs have been shopping for almost 200 years.

SPORT & ACTIVITIES

KAIYUKAN AQUARIUM (海遊館) ⭐ 🐣
This sensational aquarium is one of the biggest in the world! As well as walking through an underwater glass tunnel, you can explore the fauna and flora of diverse habitats around the Pacific Ocean in 14 large aquariums. If there are lots of visitors, follow the spiral path downwards as this will allow you to view each zone at three different levels: above water, just from below the waterline and also at a deeper level. Two huge whale sharks, flanked by manta rays and shoals of fish, circle in a tank. Feeding time is around 10.30am and 3pm. Sea lions, dolphins and penguins endear themselves by their playfulness. Also fascinating are the smaller tanks with jellyfish. Daily at 5pm, day turns into night – showing entirely new aspects of life under water. Daily 10am–8pm, closed at irregular times | admission 2,300 yen, children (7–15)

> **INSIDER TIP**
> Changing light and marine species

1,200 yen, (4–6) 600 yen | 1-1-10 Kaigandori, Minato-ku | 港区海岸通 *1-1-10 | kaiyukan.com/language/ english |* ⏱ *3 hrs*

UNIVERSAL STUDIOS JAPAN (ユニバーサルスタジオジャパン) 🎠

Seen enough temples? Then go and have fun in this theme park based on famous film series such as *Jurassic Park, Harry Potter* and *Spiderman*. Get your adrenaline kick on the roller-coaster and refresh at whitewater attractions. *Daily changing opening hours, at the earliest from 8.30am, closed by 9pm at the latest | admission 7,400 yen, children 5,100 yen (day tickets) | 2-1-33 Sakurajima, Konohana-ku |* 此花区桜島*2-1-33 | usj.co.jp/e | Universal City railway station |* ⏱ *4–8 hrs*

GO-KART RIDE

Adorn the costume of your favourite video game hero, get into a go-kart and whisk through Osaka's streets on a 90- to 120-minute guided ride. *Street Kart Osaka | daily noon–10pm | tour 9,000 yen | Ohiraki Souko-D-go, 3-1-10 Ohiraki, Fukushima-ku |* 福島区大開*3-1-10* 大開倉庫*D号 | kart.st/osaka*

NIGHTLIFE

The people of Osaka know how to celebrate! Choose from karaoke bars, live music venues, nightclubs and *tachinomiya* – popular bars and restaurants where you eat standing up.

Sea lion in sight!

CLUB JOULE (クラブジュール)

There is always a party here, even during the week. The club extends over three floors with dance floor, bar and lounge. Don't forget to bring you passport! *Daily 10pm–5am | admission from 1,000 yen | Minamisumiyacho Bldg. 2-4F, 2-11-7 Nishishinsaibashi, Chuo-ku |* 中央区西心斎橋*2-11-7* 南炭屋町ビル*2-4F | clubjoule.com | Shinsaibashi railway station*

ROCK ROCK (ロックロック)

Keep your eyes open for musicians who hang out in this bar after their concert! The visitor list reads like a Who's Who of the world of music: from Metallica and Green Day, Marilyn Manson to Lady Gaga! *Mon–Sat 7pm–5am, Sun 7pm–1am | Shinsaibashi Atrium 3F, 1-8-1 Nishishinsaibashi,*

Himeji Castle is widely regarded as the most beautiful castle in Japan

Chuo-ku | 中央区西心斎橋 *1-8-1* 心斎橋アトリアム *3F*

AROUND OSAKA

🔟 KOBA-SAN (高野山) ★ 🚩
90km from Osaka / 2½ hrs by train and bus

In this mountainous region, you can experience spiritual Japan and one of its most beautiful UNESCO World Heritage Sites. Deep in the densely forested mountains of Wakayama is the *Kongobu-ji*, the mother temple of Shingon Buddhism, brought to Japan by Kobo Daishi 1,200 years ago. Another 100 temples were constructed around Japan's biggest stone garden: *Banryutei*. Don't forget to visit the enormous *Okunoin Cemetery* *(daily 6am–5pm | admission free | Okunoin-mae bus station)* with Kobo Daishi's mausoleum. Stay in a temple and enjoy vegetarian monastic cuisine and morning meditation *(book at eng. shukubo.net). Koyasan World Heritage ticket 2,680 yen | ropeway from Gokurakubashi railway station, then 10 mins by bus |* 📖 *E8*

INSIDER TIP
Sleep in a temple

KOBE

(📖 E8) **Spread out between the sea and the mountains, Kobe (pop. 1.5 million) is one of the most beautifully situated cities in Japan.**

Kobe's port was one of the first to be opened up for trade with the outside world – a heritage which shows to this day in the many areas of the city. Kobe is also remembered for the devastating earthquake of 1995 – and for fine Kobe beef!

SIGHTSEEING

THE GREAT HANSHIN-AWAJI EARTHQUAKE MEMORIAL MUSEUM (阪神・淡路大震災記念・人と防災未来センター)

In 1995, just before 6am, an earthquake of magnitude 7.3 gruesomely woke people from their sleep. It and the subsequent fires left 6,400 people dead and 27,000 injured, as well as ruining 45,000 buildings. Unforgotten are the images of a motorway flyover tipped to one side. This museum tells you what exactly happened on that day, and English-speaking volunteers are happy to answer any questions. *Oct–June Tue–Sun 9.30am–5.30pm, July–Sept Sun, Tue–Thu 9am–6pm, Fri/Sat 9am–7pm | admission 600 yen | 1-5-2 Wakinohamakaigandori, Chuo-ku |* 中央区脇浜海岸通 *1-5-2 | dri.ne.jp/en | JR station Nada |* ⏱ *1½ hrs*

SHIN-KOBE ROPEWAY (新神戸ロープウェー)

From the Shinkansen station of Shin-Kobe, the ropeway takes you above wooded mountain slopes to the Rokko range where the viewing platform presents marvellous views of the city by day and night. *Daily 9.30am–5pm, at weekends until 8.30pm | return tickets 1,500 yen | JR station Shin-Kobe*

EATING & DRINKING

KOBE PLAISIR (神戸プレジール)

Book a seat at the counter and watch how the chefs prepare Kobe and Tajima beef and other delicacies for you. All ingredients are locally sourced. Not cheap *(Kobe beef menu from 11,000 yen)* but worth the money! *Tue–Sun 11.30am–3pm, 5–10.30pm | Hotel The b' Kobe 1F, 2-11-5 Shimoyamate-dori |* 央区下山手通 *2-11-5、* ホテル ザ・ビー神戸 *1F | kobeplaisir-honten.jp/english | Bhf. Sannomiya | ¥¥¥*

AROUND KOBE

14 HIMEJI CASTLE (姫路城) ★
60km from Osaka / 1 hr by train
The bright white, 400-year-old castle towers above Himeji (pop. 531,000). Regarded as the country's most beautiful castle, it has extensive grounds with more than 80 buildings and courtyards which are interconnected by winding paths. From the main building's tower you can look out across the city; its fish-shaped roof decoration is intended to protect against fire. *Sept–April daily 9am–5pm, May–Aug 9am–6pm | admission from 1,000 yen | 68 Honmachi, Himeji-shi, Hyogo-ken |* 兵庫県姫路市本町 *68 | city.himeji.lg.jp/guide/castle_en.html | JR station Himeji |* ⏱ *1½ hrs |* ⏛ *E8*

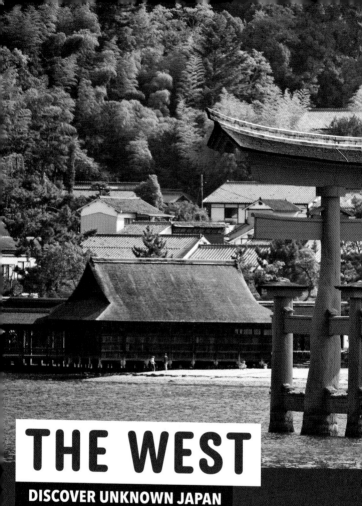

THE WEST

DISCOVER UNKNOWN JAPAN

The only city in Western Japan that is reasonably well known outside the country is Hiroshima. Other towns in the Chugoku region and on Shikoku, Japan's fourth biggest island, are rarely visited by travellers.

Those who explore the region by ferry, bus, slow train or hire car off the beaten tourist track will have the temples, castles, shrines and samurai residences almost to themselves. This is because these sites aren't on the Shinkansen routes.

The eye-catching, bright red gate on the Miyajima Shrine Island

The effort of travelling here is rewarded with diverse natural habitats from sand dunes and limestone caves in the coastal landscapes of the Seto Inland Sea to the densely forested mountain valleys on Shikoku or in the hinterland of Okayama and Tottori. The people here are extremely hospitable and helpful. The attractions of Western Japan are its quietness and the possibility of genuine exploration.

THE WEST

Izumo-Taisha ★ 5
Izumo 出雲市
Ōda City 大田市
9
Omori ★
p. 113

Kawamoto 川本町
Ohnan 邑南町
Kitahiroshima 北広島町
110km, 2½hrs
74
Akitakata 安芸高田市

Sea of Japan

Masuda 益田市
9
Akiota 安芸太田町

Abu 阿武町
Tsuwano 6

Nagato 長門市
9
● Hagi
p. 114
Yoshika 吉賀町

Hiroshima Peace Memorial Park ★
30km, 1 hr
● Hiroshima
p. 106

Mine 美祢市
29km, 1 hr, 10mins
7 Akiyoshido limestone cave ★
2 Miyajima ★

Yamaguchi 山口市
Iwakuni 岩国市
Kure 呉市

Shunan 周南市
2
Hikari 光市
Suo-Oshima 周防大島町
2

Ube 宇部市
Kaminoseki 上関町
Dogo Onsen ★
Matsuyama 松山市

Kanda 苅田町
Aki-nada 安芸灘

10
Bungo Takada 豊後高田市
Ikata 伊方町
Uchiko 内子町

Yoshitomi 吉富町
Kunisaki 国東市
56

97
Kitsuki 杵築市
Seiyo 西予市

Kusu 玖珠町
● Beppu 別府市

MARCO POLO HIGHLIGHTS

★ **KORAKU-EN**
Cherry and plum trees, rice plants and tea shrubs around a pond – this garden is Japan in miniature ➤ p. 104

★ **KURASHIKI**
Jeans "made in Japan" are fashionable – and this is where they are produced ➤ p. 104

★ **DOGO ONSEN**
Relax in the spa of spirits and deities ➤ p. 106

★ **HIROSHIMA PEACE MEMORIAL PARK**
A worthwhile and moving place to visit ➤ p. 106

MIYAJIMA
The shrine island with a big red gate offshore is one of the most photographed locations in Japan ➤ p. 109

IZUMO-TAISHA
At this "lover's shrine", the gods will help you find a partner ➤ p. 112

OMORI
Travel back in time to one of Japan's most beautiful villages ➤ p. 113

AKIYOSHIDO LIMESTONE CAVE
Explore the biggest limestone caves in the country with their underground waterfalls ➤ p. 115

OKAYAMA

(□ D8) **The old castle city (pop. 720,000) is mainly known for its marvellous *Koraku-en landscape garden*.**

In Okayama, gourmets enjoy *kaki-oko*, hearty Japanese pancakes with oysters *(kaki)*, and locally grown white peaches for dessert. Fashion lovers mustn't miss a trip to neighbouring Kurashiki, birthplace of Japanese jeans. Okayama is also the departure point for trains, ferries and hire cars to Shikoku Island.

SIGHTSEEING

OKAYAMA CASTLE (岡山城)

Its dark exterior has given this castle its nickname of "crow's nest". Only one building remains from its foundation period in the 15/16th centuries; the rest was reconstructed after World War II. On the inside, the concrete building is unspectacular, but you can try on kimonos for free. In the evening, when the castle is beautifully illuminated, the Asahi River romantically reflects its image. *Daily 9am–5.30pm, closed 29–31 Dec | admission 300 yen, 560 yen incl. Koraku-en | 2-3-1 Marunouchi, Kita-ku|北区丸の内2-3-1|okayama-kanko.net/ujo/english/index.html | Kencho-mae bus station*

INSIDER TIP
City, castle & river

KORAKU-EN (後楽園) ★ ▐

One of Japan's loveliest gardens was created as early as 1687, with the neighbouring Okayama Castle forming a part of the panorama. The garden has a typically Japanese feel, with plum, cherry and maple trees, tea shrubs and rice fields. *Daily 20 March–Sept 7.30am–6pm, Oct–19 March 8am–5pm | admission 400 yen, 560 yen incl. castle | 1-5 Korakuen, Kita-ku | 北区後楽園1-5 | okayama-korakuen. jp/english | Korakuen-mae bus station*

AROUND OKAYAMA

1 KURASHIKI ★ (倉敷市)

17km from Okayama / 17 mins by train

During the Edo period, rice was stored and distributed in Kurashiki (pop. 482,000). Make sufficient time for a stroll through the historic quarter of Kurashiki Bikan alongside a willow-lined canal. Many of the old rice storage buildings have been turned into museums, boutiques and cafés. The *Ohara Museum (Tue–Sun 9am–5pm | admission 1,300 yen | 1-1-15 Chuo, Kurashiki-shi, Okayama-ken | ohara. or.jp/en | JR station Okayama)* delights with its small but fine collection of paintings by Western masters such as El Greco, Gauguin, Monet and Matisse.

The Kojima quarter, where denim was first produced in Japan, is a mecca for jeans fans from all over the world *(okayamadenim.com/pages/about-kojima)*. The global Momotaro brand has a shop here *(daily 10am–7pm | 1-12-17 Kojima-Ajino, Kurashiki-shi)*. □ D8

Artists cherish Kurashiki's historic quarter

SHIKOKU

(◫ C9–D8) **Japan's fourth largest island is one of its least developed regions.**

For a long time, the island, which comprises the prefectures of Kagawa, Tokushima, Kochi and Ehime, was only accessible by ferry from the main island of Honshu. However, since the completion in 1988 of the Seto-Ohashi, a two-floor bridge-and-viaduct combination, getting to Shikoku has become much easier and faster.

Shikoku is predominantly known for the pilgrimage through the mountainous and wooded interior to 88 temples around the island. The 1,200km long route leads through the four prefecture capitals of Tokushima, Kochi, Matsuyama and Takamatsu – sadly often on heavily frequented coastal roads. The pilgrimage can be traced back to Dobo Daishi, the monk who introduced Shingon Buddhism to Japan in the eighth century. The typical pilgrim's outfit is in his memory: a white waistcoat, conical hat and wooden walking stick. The focus is on walking in quiet reflection, but there are many organised tours of the route, including by bus, that take a more secular approach.

SIGHTSEEING

TAKAMATSU (高松市)
This port city (pop. 420,000) in Japan's smallest prefecture of Kagawa is a good starting point for reaching the islands in the Seto Inland Sea. The

Ritsurin-koen landscape garden (daily 7am–5pm, longer in summer | admission 410 yen, audio guide hire 200 yen | 11-20-16 Ritsurin-cho, Takamatsu-shi, Kagawa-ken | my-kagawa.jp/en/ritsurin | JR station Ritsurinkoen-Kitaguchi | ☉ 3 hrs) will enchant you with a view from a hill across ponds, bridges and pavilions. Take a break in the *Kikugetsu-tei Tea House* and enjoy a cup of tea on the veranda. *ᒫ D8*

MATSUYAMA (松山市) ⚑

Well-preserved Matsuyama Castle towers on a hill above the city of the same name (pop. 510,000), with fabulous views of the Seto Inland Sea. Relax in the popular ★ *Dogo Onsen* resort *(dogo.jp/en)* at the northeastern edge of the city, one of the oldest hot spring resorts in Japan. The 1894 *Dogo Onsen Honkan* main bathhouse *(daily 6am–11pm | admission 410–1,550 yen | ☉ 2 hrs)* allows you to bathe in two pools, segregated for men and women: the Bath of the Gods and the Bath of the Spirits. Have you seen the animated film *Spirited Away* by director Hayao Miyazaki? The bathhouse of the witch Yubaba in the film is said to have been inspired by the *Dogo Onsen*, with its labyrinth of corridors, stairs and rooms. The resort is undergoing renovations until at least 2025, so not all of its areas are accessible. *Dogo Onsen tram station | ᒫ K8*

INSIDER TIP
Don't be afraid of the witch's house

HIROSHIMA

(ᒫ D8) **Located on six river tributaries, this "metropolis by the water" (pop. 1.2 million) is an important transport hub.**

Over the centuries, a lively city developed around the castle, which dates from 1589. Then, on 6 August 1945, at 8.15am, the US bomber "Enola Gay" dropped the first atom bomb in history on the city. As a result, tens of thousands of people suffered an instant death, with more than 140,000 people dead by the end of the year. The survivors have since told their stories to keep the memory of these events alive, and Hiroshima's mayors have campaigned for global nuclear disarmament.

SIGHTSEEING

HIROSHIMA PEACE MEMORIAL PARK (平和記念公園) ★

In the location where the atom bomb extinguished the heart of the city is

WHERE TO START?

Hiroshima is one of the few cities in Japan with a tram network (Hiroshima Dentetsu). Just board a tram to get to the Peace Memorial Park. In order to ride to Miyajima Island, you first need to return to the main railway station. From there, take the JR train to Miyajimaguchi (San-yo line) and continue by ferry.

A colourful message: origami cranes in Hiroshima's Peace Memorial Park

now a large riverside park with several memorials for the victims in various spots, as well as relics from that time.

The famous *Atomic Bomb Dome (daily around the clock | admission free | visithiroshima.net/world_heritage/a_ bomb_dome | Genbaku-domu-mae tram station)* is a UNESCO World Heritage Site. Despite the atomic bomb exploding almost directly above this former chamber of industry and commerce, the building's thick walls absorbed the shock waves and remained intact while everything inside caught fire.

The *Memorial Cenotaph* contains a list of the victims who died – with the inscription: "Let all the souls here rest in peace for we shall not repeat the evil". The *Peace Flame*, on a monument designed by architect Kenzo Tange to resemble human hands, has been burning since 1964. It is intended to extinguish only when there are no more nuclear weapons. The *Peace Bell* is surrounded by a lotus flower pond – you can ring it to promote peace.

You should also visit the *Children's Peace Monument*, constructed for Sadako Sasaki. According to a Japanese legend, anyone who folds 1,000 origami cranes will be granted a wish by the gods. In this way, 12-year-old Sasaki, who suffered from radiation poisoning, hoped to beat her cancer. However, the girl died just before she completed the task. Since then, many visitors have left strings of folded cranes by the monument in her memory. *Daily around the clock | admission free | Heiwa-koen-mae bus station*

A dream in pink with a red gate to another world: the shrine on Miyajima Island

HIROSHIMA PEACE MEMORIAL MUSEUM
(平和記念資料館) 🎏

This museum, designed by well-known Japanese architect Kenzo Tange, opened ten years after the atomic bomb was dropped on Hiroshima. Various simulated settings and relics, such as molten bottles and coins, attempt to hit home the apocalyptic scale of the destruction, accompanied by both written and visual witness reports. The museum explains the consequences of the radioactive radiation in detail and promotes the abolition of all nuclear weapons. *March–July, Sept–Nov daily 8.30am–6pm, Aug 8.30am–7pm, Dec–Feb 8.30am–5.30pm | admission 200 yen | 1-2 Nakajimacho, Naka-ku |* 中区中島町 *1-2 | hpmmuseum.jp/?lang=eng | Heiwa-kinen-koen bus station*

MAZDA MUSEUM
(マツダミュージアム) 🎏🐗

The Japanese car maker Mazda, founded in 1920, has remained loyal to its hometown of Hiroshima, with more than one million cars rolling off the production line here every year. A free 90-minute tour shows you a part of the production area and the company's museum. *Daily from 10am, book via the website, admission free | mazda.com/en/about/museum | Mukainada railway station*

EATING & DRINKING

MICCHAN SOU-HONTEN
(みっちゃん 総本店)

Okonomiyaki, Hiroshima-style, consists of a thin dough onto which ingredients such as cabbage, spring onions, sprouts, pork and – in contrast to Osaka – wheat noodles are layered. On top is a layer of egg with a sweet and spicy sauce and seaweed flakes. Although this may sound a little strange to Western palates, it is actually delicious – and the soul food of this region! As an option, you can order oysters to go with it, another speciality. *Thu–Tue 11am–2.30pm, 5.30–9.30pm | 1F Churis Hatchobori, 6-7 Hatchobori, Naka-ku |* 中区八丁堀6-7 チュリス八丁堀1F *| Hatchobori tram station |* ¥

illuminated until 11pm. Take comfortable shoes with you, because a trip to the mountain peak by ropeway is recommended. With a bit of luck, you can even spot wild monkeys. The return journey is either by ropeway or – if you schedule sufficient time – on hiking trails past an eternal flame. If you stay overnight in a *ryokan*, you will have enough time for everything, deer watching on the shore included. *C8*

INSIDER TIP
Sleep on the holy island

AROUND HIROSHIMA

☑ MIYAJIMA (宮島) ★

30km from Hiroshima / 1 hr by train and ferry

The small island of Miyajima ("Shrine Island") is one of the country's most popular travel destinations. It is known, in particular, for the big orange-red *torii* gate which seems to float above the water at high tide, marking the entrance to the *Itsukushima-jinja Shrine (March–14 Oct daily 6.30am–6pm, Jan–Feb and 15 Oct–Nov 6.30am–5.30pm, Dec 6.30am–5pm | admission from 300 yen | Miyajima-guchi railway station | ⏱ 30 mins)*, which was founded in 1168. But don't worry: the shrine is accessible from dry land on shoreline paths. If you are keen to get your feet in the water, wait for low tide when you can walk through the gate.

The shrine's magical beauty is

MATSUE

(D7) **Off the Shinkansen routes in the Shimane Prefecture by the Sea of Japan, you will discover a country far from the tourist trail which offers incredible sights that are just as worth seeing as those in better known regions.**

Shimane's capital Matsue (pop. 202,000) on the shores of Lake Shinji-ko is the ideal starting point for trips to the surrounding countryside. However, the laid back city itself has a lot to offer, including an intact castle and a pretty samurai quarter. *Matsue Goodwill Guides (free guided tours, but you pay for the transport | book at info@kankou-matsue.jp)* provide English-speaking tours to local destinations.

SIGHTSEEING

MATSUE CASTLE (松江城)

This is one of only a dozen Japanese

castles that have remained in their original state. Known as the "Black Castle" because of its dark wooden construction materials, it is located on a hill and hidden behind thick stone walls. 🐾 You can explore the moat by boat *(Horikawa Sightseeing Boat | every 20–30 mins 9am–4pm | 50 mins ride | tickets 1,200 yen, children (6 12) 600 yen | matsue-horikawameguri.jp).* In the castle you can admire old weapons, samurai armour and musical instruments. The steep wooden stairs will get you fit! North of the castle is a pretty quarter with a samurai residence *(opening times same as castle | admission 300 yen | 305 Shiomi-Nawate, Kitahori-cho | ⏱ 30 mins)* and appealing artisan shops. *April–Sept daily 8.30am–6.30pm, Oct–March 8.30am–5pm | admission 280 yen | 1-5 Tonomachi | Kokuho-matsuejo-kenchozen bus station | ⏱ 1 hr*

FESTIVAL

SUMMER FIREWORKS
(松江水郷祭湖上花火大会)
In Japan, summer is fireworks season, and one of the most impressive displays is staged in Matsue. Launched from two locations, the result are fascinating symmetries in the sky. In addition, the "fire flowers" *(hana-bi)* – as fireworks are known in Japanese – are reflected in the lake. The oohs and aahs uttered by the spectators are rather infectious. Enjoy the festival atmosphere, with many food stalls and amateur wrestling competitions. *Early Aug 8–9pm | for the exact date go to visit-matsue.com.*

AROUND MATSUE

🔳 TOTTORI SAND DUNES
(鳥取砂丘) 🐾
120km from Matsue / 2 hrs by train and bus
Camel riding across the dunes – in Japan? This is a typical pastime in the Tottori sand dunes. They are not the only dunes in Japan, but they are the biggest: 16km long, up to 2km wide and 50m tall. Climbing up will give you tired legs! The dunes are the result of river sand that was once carried out to sea, from where it was washed back onto the shore by the currents and heaped up over thousands of years. You can swim nearby at the *Tottori-Sakyu Beach Resort* near

Oasis Plaza, 3km away. As well as camel rides (*Rakudaya | March–Nov daily 9.30am–4.30pm, Dec–Feb 10am–4pm | admission 1,300 yen | near the car park at the sand dunes*), you can try sandboarding across the dunes (*Tottori-Sakyu Sandboard School, three times a day | from 3,000 yen/pers. | near the car park at the sand dunes | tssbt1.wixsite.com/tottori-sandboard*). In the nearby *Sand Museum (mid-April–Dec Sun, Fri 9am–6pm, Sat 9am–8pm | admission 600 yen | sand-museum.jp/en | Sakyu Kita-guchi bus station*) artists create new and highly detailed artworks from sand around a specific topic every year. *Daily around the clock | Yuyama, Fukube-cho, Tottori-shi, Tottori-ken | 鳥取県鳥取市福部町湯山2164-661 | Tottori Sakyu bus station | ﹏ D7*

4 ADACHI MUSEUM OF ART
(足立美術館)

23km from Matsue / 1 hr and 20 mins by train and bus

The best-known artwork in this art museum is the sophisticated garden, which changes according to the weather and the seasons, but, sadly, can only be viewed from the perimeter. It is regularly awarded for being Japan's most beautiful garden. The award-winning garden, whose bushes are clipped into perfect rounded shapes, was founded by entrepreneur Zenko Adachi, who once called himself a "reckless, charging, wild boar kind of a man". The main building exhibits artworks by Japanese painter Taikan Yokoyama, and 20th century art is displayed in an annex. *Daily April–Sept 9am–5.30pm, Oct–March 9am–5pm | admission 1,650 yen | 320*

Sahara feeling with a sea view: walk for miles across the Tottori sand dunes

Furukawa-cho, Yasugi-shi, Shimane-ken | 島根県安来市古川町320 | *adachi-museum.or.jp/en | shuttle bus from Yasugi railway station* | 🚌 D7

5 IZUMO-TAISHA (出雲大社) ★
44km from Matsue / 1½ hrs by train and bus

In Japan, the Izumo-Taisha is known as a love shrine and a powerful sacred in the middle because this space is reserved for millions of Shinto deities who congregate there every year. Also famous are the huge straw ropes at the shrine's buildings which symbolise the separation between the world of the divine and that of the mortals. Until 1744, the Izumo Taisha was rebuilt at regular intervals in accordance with Shinto tradition. Since then,

No need for a dating app: order your ideal partner at the Izumo-Taisha shrine of lovers

site. People looking for love use small wooden boards precisely to specify the personality traits of their dream partner, and the Gods look after everything else! The eighth-century shrine is one of oldest in the country and closely connected to Japan's founding myths. From a giant wooden gate at the entrance, you walk downhill until the path splits. Avoid walking comprehensive renovation work has been cut back to once every 60 years; the most recent renovation lasted from 2008 to 2013. *Shrine daily around the clock, treasury 8.30am–4.30pm | shrine admission free, treasury 300 yen | 195 Taishacho Kizukihigashi, Izumo-shi, Shimane-ken |* 島根県出雲市大社町杵築東195 | *izumo-kankou.gr.jp/english/*

4760 | bus from JR station Izumoshi | shrine ⏱ 1½ hrs | ⑈ D7

OMORI

(⑈ C7) **The small village of ★ Omori (pop. 400), which belongs to the town of Oda, is little known but one of the prettiest in the whole of Japan.**

It is a part of the UNESCO World Heritage Site around the Iwami-Ginzan silver mine with its 650 shafts, trade routes, fortifications, harbours and settlements. Not too bad for a village that was threatened with abandonment 60 years ago – until a prosthetics manufacturer created jobs on site and reconstructed the village one house at a time. Today, you'll find pretty traditional houses made of dark wood with red roofs in a bamboo-covered river valley, as well as cosy cafés, the "world's smallest opera house" and boutiques selling arts and crafts. *iwamiginzan.jp*

SIGHTSEEING

IWAMI-GINZAN SILVER MINE (石見銀山)

In 1309, silver was discovered deep in the mountains of western Japan and, in the early 1500s, a method for exploiting it was developed. In its heyday in the early 17th century, the mine produced 38 tons of silver annually – approx. one third of global silver production! However, silver deposits decreased over time, and the mine was closed down in 1923. Hundreds of thousands of people lived here in past centuries, but today the area is densely wooded, with only a few ruins and gravestones visible. The *Ryugenji Mabu* mineshaft *(March–Nov daily 9am–5pm, Dec–Feb 9am–4pm | admission 200 yen | ⏱ 20–30 mins)* is open to visitors; it's not particularly spectacular, but the 45-minute hike to get there from Omori is lovely. It is best to get local guides to explain the site to you in English *(book at info@iwamiginzan-guide.jp | tel. 0854 89 01 20).*

INSIDER TIP
Discover the area with local guides

RAKAN-JI TEMPLE (羅漢寺)

Fascinatingly lifelike: 501 statues of Buddhist monks, made by local artisans in the 18th century, are lined up in stone caves next to the temple. They are meant to comfort the souls of those who died in the silver mine. Allegedly, you will be able to discover the faces of deceased family members in the statues. *Daily 9am–5pm | temple admission free, caves 500 yen | i 804 Omori-cho, Oda-shi, Shimane-ken | 島根県大田市大森町イ804 | ⏱ 1 hr*

EATING & DRINKING

HIDAKA BAKERY & CONFECTIONERY (ベッカライ・コンディトライ・ヒダカ)

The bakery is managed by a young Japanese couple who trained in Germany. They produce fine continental pretzels and rye bread, a rarity In

Japan, in a restored traditional house. *Fri–Tue 10am–5pm | ha 90-1 Omori-cho, Oda-shi, Shimane-ken |* 島根県大田市大森町ハ90-1

SHOPPING

GUNGENDO (群言堂)

You will find it near-impossible to leave this shop without having bought something: clothes, arts and crafts, leather goods, kitchenware – they have wonderful items, many of which are regional and hand-made. Relax in the café in a courtyard full of plants. *March–Nov Thu–Tue 10am–6pm, Dec–Feb Fri–Tue 10am–6pm | 183 Omori-cho, Oda-shi, Shimane-ken |* 島根県大田市大森町ハ183

HAGI

(□ C8) **Although the castle which used to dominate Hagi (pop. 47,000) is now in ruins, this ancient town is worth discovering.**

Since 2015, five sites in Hagi have been declared UNESCO World Heritage Sites because they reflect Japan's industrial revolution during the Meiji period. Of particular interest are the residences of samurais and merchants, e.g. the cleverly designed *Kikuya Residence (daily 8.30am–5.30pm | admission 600 yen | ⏱ 45 mins)* and the 200-year old *Kubota Residence (daily 9am–5pm | admission 100 yen).*

SIGHTSEEING

TOKO-JI TEMPLE (東光寺)

Doesn't this look Chinese? Actually, yes: the temples of the Obaku school of Japanese Zen Buddhism display Chinese influences, for example at the red entrance gate. The symmetrically laid out cemetery behind it has the graves of the feudal lords of the Mori clan who ruled Hagi during the Edo period. *Daily 8.30am–5pm | admission 300 yen | 1647 Chinto, Hagi-shi, Yamaguchi-ken |* 山口県萩市椿東1647 | *Toko-ji-mae bus station*

SHOPPING

Hagi is known for *hagiyaki* ceramics which are sought after because of their clear fine lines, high-quality tea bowls and white glaze that resembles icing sugar. There are approx. 100 potteries in the town. In the *Hagiyaki-Kaikan (daily 8am–5pm | 3155 Chinto Shinkawa, Higashi-ku, Hagi-shi, Yamaguchi-ken)* you can choose from a wide selection, watch potters at work and try your hand at the potter's wheel yourself *(telephone booking on the day possible on 0838 25 95 45).*

AROUND HAGI

⑥ TSUWANO (津和野町) 🏳
55km from Hagi / 1¼ hrs by car
The small town (pop. 7,300) is known as the "little Kyoto of the San'in region".

Almost perfectly formed: pottery made in Hagi

Why? See for yourself in the picturesque Tonomachi quarter in the old town, a 10-minute walk from the railway station, with its historic walls and buildings by small carp-filled canals. Walk for another 10 minutes to the entrance of the *Taikodani Inari-jinja (daily around the clock | admission free)*, one of the five most important fox shrines. Inari is the Goddess of Fertility, Rice and Foxes, which is why foxes are regarded as sacred in Japan. You reach the shrine on a winding uphill path through 1,000 orange-red gates. The shrine was meant to protect Tsuwano Castle against evil spirits; today only the foundations remain. Visitors pray for a good harvest, wealth and happiness. ⌘ *C8*

◤ AKIYOSHIDO LIMESTONE CAVE (秋芳洞) ★☂
29km from Hagi / 1¼ hrs by bus

With the background noise of an underground river, here you'll discover the earth's history first hand. Stretching for 9km, Akiyoshido is Japan's largest limestone cave. A 1-km-long stretch is accessible to visitors on well-lit easy trails. Particularly impressive are the huge limestone terraces where water collects, as well as underground waterfalls.

The cave stretches underneath the Akiyoshidai upland plateau, which has the greatest concentration of karst rock formations in Japan and can be discovered on hiking trails. They are said to have developed from a 300-million-year-old coral reef. *Daily 8.30am–4.30pm | admission with a foreign passport 700 yen | daily two buses from Hagi (from 1,720 yen), JR Pass not valid | en.karusuto.com/spot/akiyoshido | ⌚ 4 hrs incl. hike | ⌘ C8*

THE SOUTH

VOLCANOES & THE TROPICS: JAPAN'S HOT ZONE

In southern Japan, nature is the star of the show: there are smouldering volcanoes, such as Aso or Sakurajima, idyllic coastal landscapes and fascinating coral reefs around Amami-Oshima and Okinawa.

Seen as the gateway to mainland Asia, this region also offers much to lovers of culture, not least its religious dance traditions. Kyushu comprises the prefectures of Fukuoka, Kumamoto, Nagasaki, Oita, Saga, Kagoshima and Miyazaki, stretching across hundreds of

Snorkelling fun on an Okinawa coral reef at subtropical temperatures

offshore islands. Even further south are the Okinawa Islands, Japan's subtropical bathing paradise. While it may well snow in winter on Kyushu, one of Japan's main islands, temperatures on Amami-Oshima and Okinawa almost never drop below 15°C. This is the place for anyone in search of a bit of culture, lots of nature and plenty of relaxation. Even today, Okinawa feels like a world apart from the rest of the country; nowhere else are the Japanese more easy-going and approachable than in this former kingdom.

THE SOUTH

Odika
小値賀町

Gotô
五島市

275 km, 1 hr, 35 mins

MARCO POLO HIGHLIGHTS

★ **ASO**
Hikers will love the mega-caldera of the active Aso volcano ➤ p. 124

★ **TAKACHIHO GORGE**
Beautiful nature, closely linked to Japan's mythology ➤ p. 125

★ **NAGASAKI ATOMIC BOMB MUSEUM**
An excellent and impressive exhibition: learn from history and then become a part of the movement for peace ➤ p. 126

★ **GUNKANJIMA**
Fascinating ruins on a former coal mine island that even James Bond has visited ➤ p. 129

★ **SAKURAJIMA**
Experience the earth's history in action around one of Japan's most active volcanoes ➤ p. 130

★ **YAKUSHIMA**
Unspoilt nature: beaches, ancient forest and mountains that are almost 2,000m high ➤ p. 132

★ **WHALE WATCHING OFF OKINAWA**
Get a close look at these large marine mammals on a boat tour ➤ p. 134

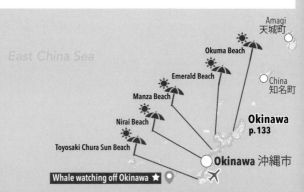

East China Sea

Amagi
天城町

Okuma Beach

Emerald Beach

China
知名町

Manza Beach

Okinawa
p. 133

Nirai Beach

Toyosaki Chura Sun Beach

Okinawa 沖縄市

Whale watching off Okinawa ★

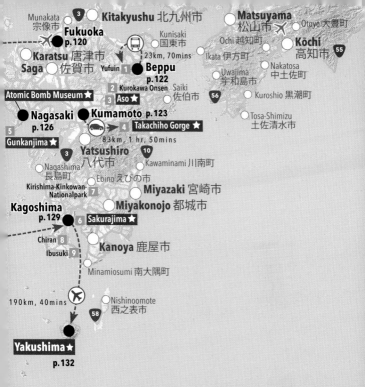

Munakata 宗像市

3

Kitakyushu 北九州市

Matsuyama 松山市

Otoyo 大豊町

✈ **Fukuoka** p. 120

Kunisaki 国東市

Ochi 越知町

Kōchi 高知市

55

Karatsu 唐津市

Ikata 伊方町

23km, 70mins

Nakatosa 中土佐町

Saga 佐賀市

Yufuin 1

Beppu p. 122

Uwajima 宇和島市

Kuroshio 黒潮町

Kurokawa Onsen 2

56

Saiki 佐伯市

★ **Atomic Bomb Museum** ★

Aso ★ 3

Nagasaki p. 126

Kumamoto p. 123

Tosa-Shimizu 土佐清水市

4 **Takachiho Gorge** ★

5

83km, 1 hr, 50mins

Gunkanjima ★

Yatsushiro 八代市

3

10

Nagashima 長島町

Kawaminami 川南町

Kirishima-Kinkowan-Nationalpark

Ebino えびの市 7

Miyazaki 宮崎市

Miyakonojo 都城市

Kagoshima p. 129

6 **Sakurajima** ★

Chiran 8

Kanoya 鹿屋市

Ibusuki 9

Minamiosumi 南大隅町

✈ 190km, 40mins

Nishinoomote 西之表市

58

Yakushima ★ p. 132

PACIFIC OCEAN

Tatsugo 龍郷町

Kikai 喜界町

▲

100 km
62.15 mi

FUKUOKA

(⊞ B8) **The biggest city (pop. 1.6 million) on Kyushu, the main island in Southern Japan, has one of the country's most important cruise ship ports. Fukuoka is known for being cosmopolitan, innovative and laid back.**

Fukuoka is only a 40-minute flight from South Korea. Due to its proximity to mainland Asia, this region has always been the gateway to Japan. In the 13th century, the Mongols attempted to conquer Japan from here but, according to legend, "divine winds" *(kamikaze)* prevented an invasion.

SIGHTSEEING

NANZO-IN (南蔵院)

You cannot miss this temple's highlight: the world's biggest statue of the reclining Buddha is as tall as six men, as long as 20 men and as heavy as a jumbo jet. It depicts the Buddha shortly before he achieved nirvana. Five coloured ribbons are attached to his hand, and believers hold them while praying in the hope that the Buddha's power will be transferred to them. *Daily around the clock | admission free | 1035 Sasaguri, Kasuya-gun |* 糟屋郡篠栗町大字篠栗*1035* | *Kido-Nanzoin-mae railway station*

DAIZAIFU TENMAN-GU (太宰府天満宮)

The shrine's garden with its ponds and bridges has 6,000 plum trees that flower in January. It is dedicated to Michizane Sugawara, an influential ninth century politician and scholar of Chinese literature who, after his death, was declared the God of Learning. The Honden main building was last rebuilt in 1591. **INSIDER TIP** **Divine assistance** If one of your friends or children is facing an important exam, give them a lucky charm souvenir! *Sun–Thu depending on the seasons at least 6.30am–6.30pm, Fri–Sat 6.30am–8.30pm | admission free | 4-7-1 Saifu, Dazaifu-shi |* 太宰府市宰府*4-7-1* | *dazaifutenmangu.or.jp/en | Dazaifu railway station*

KYUSHU NATIONAL MUSEUM (九州国立博物館) 🌂

Japan's fourth National Museum opened in 2005, not far from the Dazaifu Shrine It is designed in the shape of a wave and documents the cultural exchange with mainland Asia in an easy-to-understand manner. The exhibits include 3,000-year-old clay figurines, gifts brought by Chinese and Korean envoys, as well as swords and precious tea bowls. You may touch selected original items and watch the restorers at work. *Tue–Thu, Sun 9.30am–5pm, Fri/Sat 9.30am–8pm | admission 430 yen | 4-7-2 Ishizaka, Dazaifu-shi |* 太宰府市石坂*4-7-2* | *kyuhaku.jp/en | Dazaifu railway station*

EATING & DRINKING

YATAI (屋台) 🚩

Popular *yatai* food stalls only have space for small numbers of dining.

Reclining Buddha: the Nanzo-in is as heavy as a jumbo jet

Yatai can be found throughout Fukuoka, but there is a particularly large number by the water at the southern end of Nakasu Island. The dishes are simple, filling and cheap, e.g. *yakitori* chicken skewers or various ingredients stewed in a soy broth *(oden)*. They also sell alcohol. *Daily approx. 6pm–2am, some are closed on Sun | Nakasu Kawabata railway station | ¥*

HAKATA IPPUDO (博多一風堂)

The chain's history began with a single outlet in Hakata in 1985: now Ippudo can be found in a dozen countries. The menu includes the local speciality Hakata-Ramen, a hearty noodle soup with a broth made from pig bones that have been boiled for hours, plus thinly sliced roast pork, spring onions and other toppings. *Mon–Thu 11am–11pm,* *Fri 11am–midnight, Sat 10.30am–midnight, Sun 10.30am–11pm | 1-13-14 Daimyo, Chuo-ku | 中央区大名 1-13-14 | Fukuoka-Tenjin railway station | ¥*

SHOPPING

CANAL CITY
(キャナルシティ博多)

This huge and brightly colourful shopping street is a "city within the city", with 250 shops, cafés and restaurants, a theatre, cinemas and hotels. Every half-hour you can enjoy a water show in the middle of the canal. *Daily approx. 10am–9pm depending on the shop, restaurants 11am–11pm | 1-2 Sumiyoshi, Hakata-ku | 博多区住吉 1-2 | canalcity.co.jp/english | 15 mins on foot from Hakata railway station*

FESTIVALS

HAKATA GION YAMAKASA (博多祇園山笠) 🏳

Wet fun: in the first half of July, teams from seven neighbourhoods in the Hakata quarter race each other by dragging colourfully decorated floats along the road. To minimise drag, water is splashed onto the street – and onto the participants! They practise from 10 to 14 July; then, from 1am on 15 July, the teams set up at the *Kushida-jinja Shrine (daily 4am–10pm | admission free|1-41 Kamikawabata-machi, Hakata-ku | Gion railway station)*, one of the oldest in Japan. The actual kick-off is at sunrise just before 5am. If you drink from the spring with three crane statues, you and your loved ones are promised eternal youth and longevity.

BEPPU

(⧉ C9) **Steam is rising everywhere and a sulphuric smell is in the air: Beppu (pop. 117,000) is one of the best-known hot spring resorts in Japan.**

Sadly, the city on the slopes around Beppu Bay has seen better days, but it is still worth visiting because of the eight springs from which more thermal waters bubble than anywhere else in the island nation.

SIGHTSEEING

JIGOKU (地獄)

Do not jump straight in – some bubble away at 100°C, while another is home to 80 crocodiles! These hot springs,

A hot and healing bath, but don't jump straight in!

five in the Kannawa district and another two in Shibaseki, are very popular with tourists. They are called "hells" for good reason. You can see a red "blood pond", a cobalt-blue "sea hell" and a hot water fountain. *Daily 8am–5pm | admission 400 yen/spring or 2,000 yen for all | 5 hells at Kannawa bus station and 2 at Shibaseki bus station*

EATING & DRINKING

JIGOKU-MUSHI-KOBO KANNAWA (地獄蒸し工房鉄輪) 🐷

Cook your own lunch – even if you can't cook! For *Jigoku-Mushi* (dishes steamed in hell) simply put all of the ingredients in a saucepan or bamboo basket and wait 10–30 minutes. Everything else is done by the hot steam which emerges from the earth's interior, its minerals producing a unique taste. It's a centuries-old cooking method! *Daily 9am–9pm, except for 3rd Wed of each month | steam oven fee from 340 yen for 20 mins, further 10 mins 150 yen, foodstuffs from 150 yen | 5 Furonomoto, Beppu-shi, Oita-ken | 大分県別府市風呂本5組*

WELLNESS

TANAYU (棚湯)

This spa on the roof of the relatively modern *Suginoi Hotel* offers panoramic views of the Bay of Beppu. Areas are segregated for each sex; naked bathing takes place on five partially covered terraces but, in the adjacent *Aqua Garden*, you are

obliged to wear swimming costumes. Tattooed bathers are not permitted. *Daily 9am–11pm | admission Mon–Fri 1,200 yen, Sat/Sun 1,800 yen | 1 Kankaiji Beppu-shi, Oita-ken | 大分県別府市観海寺1*

AROUND BEPPU

🔟 YUFUIN (由布院)
23km from Beppu / 2 hrs and 10 mins by bus

The hinterland of Beppu is quieter with nice cafés and shops along the main road. Surrounded by rice fields and farmhouses, Mount Yufu watches over the many *ryokan* hostels with their hot springs, e.g. the *Tsuka no Ma ryokan (444-3 Yufuin-cho, Kawakami, Yufu-shi, Oita-ken | 5 mins from the centre by taxi)*, which is an old farmhouse. 🗺 *C9*

KUMAMOTO

(🗺 B9) **The old castle city (pop. 740,000) in the centre of Kyushu is on the Shinkansen route between Fukuoka and Kagoshima and a good place for discovering the Aso volcano.**

Kumamoto suffered a strong earthquake in April 2016 but has now recovered. Its mascot is *kumamon*, a black bear with red cheeks, famous throughout Japan.

SIGHTSEEING

KUMAMOTO CASTLE (熊本城)

This majestic castle overlooks an extensive park filled with 800 cherry trees. Founded in 1607, it was rebuilt several times. It was damaged by the strong earthquake of 2011 and its ongoing reconstruction is scheduled to last 20 years. The *Honmaru-Goten Palace (April–Oct daily 8.30am–6pm, Nov–March 8.30am–5pm | admission 500 yen | 1-1 Honmaru, Chuo-ku | Kumamotojo-mae tram station | ⌚ 1 hr)* in the castle grounds is a reconstruction of the original building, which was three times the size and decorated with lots of gilt and paintings. *Daily around the clock | admission free | 1-1 Honmaru, Chuo-ku | 中央区本丸1-1 | kumamoto-guide.jp/kumamoto-castle/en/admission | Kumamotojo-mae tram station | ⌚ 1 hr*

SHOPPING

SAKURA-NO-BABA JOSAIEN (桜の馬場 城彩苑)

Stroll along this shopping street, where local specialties such as cod roe, mustard-filled lotus roots and traditional sweets are sold. It is located below the castle and features Edo-style architecture – somewhat touristy but nevertheless tasteful. *Shops March–Nov daily 9am–7pm, Dec–Feb 9am–6pm, restaurants 11am–7pm | 1-1-1 Ninomaru, Chuo-ku | 中央区二の丸1-1-1 | sakuranobaba-johsaien.jp/english*

AROUND KUMAMOTO

2 KUROKAWA ONSEN (黒川温泉)

73km from Kumamoto / 1 hr and 20 mins by car

This bathing town is 20km north of the Aso volcano in a wooded river valley. You'll hear the gushing noises of the water from the many open-air spas *(rotemburo)*. After having enjoyed a bath, you can easily spend your yen in pretty shops and cafés. *kurokawaonsen.or.jp/eng_new | ▢ C9*

3 ASO (阿蘇山) ★

50km from Kumamoto / 1 hr and 40 mins by train and bus

Would you like to live in a caldera? This is exactly what many farmers are doing in the centre of Kyushu. With a 25-km diameter and 100-km circumference, the Aso caldera is one the biggest on earth. In its centre is the active *Nakadake* volcano *(kyusanko.co.jp/aso/lang_en | from Aso railway station to the Kusasenri Aso Kazan Hakubutsukan-mae bus station and from there by cable car)*. Enquire in advance because, depending on the gas release, access may be blocked *(up-to-date safety notes at aso.ne.jp/~volcano/eng/index.html)*. Do not visit the caldera edge if you suffer from asthma, bronchitis or heart disease or if you feel ill on the day. If you smell volcanic gas, press a wet handkerchief against your mouth and nose, and move away from the edge. Several hiking trails *(from 90 mins)* lead across the grassy Kusasenri plateau, where cows and horses graze, to Mount Eboshi (1,337m) or Mount Kishimadake (1,321m). *Kusasenri-gahama, Aso-shi, Kumamoto-ken |* 熊本県阿蘇市草千里ヶ浜)| *C9*

Minainotaki waterfall, you can refresh yourself in its spray *(boat rides 8.30am–5pm | 2,000 yen/boat, max. 3 people/30 mins). Daily around the clock, in summer illuminated until 10pm |*

INSIDER TIP
What about a shower?

Hike past the "fiery mouth" of the Aso volcano

4 TAKACHIHO GORGE
(高千穂峡) ★ 🚩

83km from Kumamoto / 1 hr and 50 mins by car

The narrow gorge by the Gokase River, flanked by vertical basalt columns, is not just a beauty spot but also closely linked with Japan's divine myths, which is why it is regarded as a particularly powerful sacred site. While you can also admire the gorge from the top, the best views are from a boat. If you take the route past the

Ooaza Mitai Oshioi, Takachiho-cho, Nishiusuki-gun, Miyazaki-ken | 宮崎県西臼杵郡高千穂町大字三田井御塩井 | *30 mins on foot from Takachiho bus center, buses only run at weekends |* C9

The *Takachiho-jinja* Shrine is 1km from the gorge, surrounded by cedar trees. Every evening a dance and music performance is held in honour of the Shinto Goddess Amaterasu *(daily 8–9pm |*

INSIDER TIP
Entertaining the gods

admission 700 yen | 1037 Ooaza Mitai, Takachiho-cho, Nishiusuki-gun, Miyazaki-ken | 15 mins on foot from Takachiho bus center). Great fun even if you don't speak Japanese! ⌑ *C9*

NAGASAKI

(⌑ *B9*) **One of the most attractive cities in Japan (pop. 417,000) is located in a picturesque bay. Nagasaki has international flair and is popular with cruise-ship travellers.**

Due to its geographical location, the capital of the prefecture of the same name used to be one of Japan's most important gateways to the outside world. In the mid-1500s, the first Christian missionaries arrived here, but soon they and all converted Christians were persecuted mercilessly. The port area still features historical evidence of its foreign inhabitants during and after the Edo period in the form of churches, parks and villas. Nagasaki is also known for having been the second city on which the US dropped an atomic bomb.

WHERE TO START?

Nagasaki is one of few cities in Japan with a tram network: ideal for getting to the Peace Park and Atomic Bomb Museum. The tram also takes you to the port area with its historic churches, parks and villas.

Today tangible evidence of this dreadful event is on display in the city's Atomic Bomb Museum and the tragedy is memorialised in the Peace Park.

SIGHTSEEING

PEACE PARK (長崎平和公園)

On 9 August 1945, the "Fat Man" bomb, which was intended to destroy the Mitsubishi factories by the port 2km away, instead distributed its devastating power in the hills further north: more than 70,000 people had died by the end of 1945. Start your visit at the 10m tall *Peace Statue (daily around the clock | admission free | Matsuyamamachi | 松山町 | Heiwakoen tram station)*, which represents a huge sitting man. One arm, pointing to the sky, warns of the threat posed by nuclear weapons. The other arm, stretched to the side, is symbolic of the wish for peace, and the slightly shut eyes express contemplation of the victims. Close by is the *Bakushinchi-Koen*, which marks the hypocentre in the form of a simple, black stone monolith surrounded by stone circles. On the edge of the park, what was left of the *Urakami-Tenshudo Cathedral (daily around the clock | admission free | Matsuyamamachi | 松山町 | Heiwakoen tram station)* was reconstructed in its original location.

ATOMIC BOMB MUSEUM (長崎原爆資料館) ★ 👕

A modern glass dome marks the entrance to the excellent exhibition, which features numerous remains from the bombing, such as a pocket watch which stopped at 11.02am, the exact time when the atomic bomb was dropped. Its awesome power is demonstrated by molten rosaries and twisted bits of metal. Next door is the *Memorial Hall for the Victims (daily 8.30am–6.30pm | admission free)*, an underground construction of twelve illuminated glass pillars, their light symbolising the hope for peace. Above ground is a basin which is illuminated at night by 70,000 lights in memory of the dead. *May–Aug daily 8.30am–6.30pm, Sept–April 8.30am–5.30pm | admission 200 yen | 7-8 Hirano-machi | 平野町 7-8 | Atomic Bomb Museum/Hamaguchi-machi tram station | ⏱ 1½–2 hrs*

DEJIMA (出島)

Constructed in 1636, the man-made island of Dejima was Japan's only point of contact with Europe for more than 200 years. Initially Portuguese missionaries were isolated on the island, and later on Dutch merchants. Today, you can stroll through the reconstructed residences and warehouses. Apart from walls and gates, a section of the moat has also been rebuilt – it is nicely Illuminated in the evening. *Daily 8am–9pm | admission 510 yen | 6-1 Dejima-machi | 出島町 6-1 | nagasakidejima.jp/en | Dejima tram station | ⏱ 1–1½ hrs*

OURA CHURCH (大浦天主堂)

The basilica from 1864 is the oldest existing Catholic church in Japan and was declared a UNESCO World Heritage Site in 2018. It was built by French priests in memory of 26 martyrs who were executed during the Edo period. The museum educates visitors about the persecution of Christians in Japan. *Daily 8am–6pm | admission incl. museum 1,000 yen | 5-3 Minamiyamatemachi | 南山手町 5-3 | Oura-tenshudo-shita tram station | ⏱ 1½ hrs*

Marvellous views of Nagasaki from Inasa-yama, a popular dating spot

GLOVER GARDEN (グラバー園)

In the past, Western merchants lived in the area around Glover Garden with its harbour view. Several of their residences have been reconstructed in the garden. If you love opera, you can trace the story of *Madame Butterfly*, which takes place in Nagasaki and was made famous by Puccini's opera of the same name. *Nov–mid-July 8am–8.30pm, mid-July–Oct 8am–9.30pm | admission 610 yen | 8-1 Minamiyamatemachi | 南山手町 8-1 | glover-garden.jp/english | Oura-tenshudo-shita tram station |* ⏱ *1–1½ hrs*

INASA-YAMA VIEWPOINT (稲佐山)

Nagasaki is proud of the night-time view of the city, glittering with countless lights, from the 333-m tall Mount Inasa-yama, which is regarded as one of the three most beautiful views in the country. The *Nagasaki Ropeway* (cable car) takes you there in just five minutes. You'll enjoy 360-degree views and, in good weather, you may even spot the offshore Goto Islands. *Daily 9am–10pm, closed early Dec, cable car runs every 15–20 mins | single tickets 720 yen, return tickets 1,230 yen | 364 Inasamachi | 稲佐町 364 | Takaramachi tram station*

EATING & DRINKING

SHIKAIRO (四海楼)

In the late 1800s, the owner's great-grandfather came to Nagasaki from southern China with the idea of creating a dish that was both filling and nutritious. The result was the famous *Nagasaki-Champon* – a hearty noodle soup with vegetables, mushrooms, pork and fish cakes. *Daily 11.30am–3pm, 5–9pm | 4-5 Matsugae machi | 松が枝町4-5 | Oura-tenshudo-shita tram station | ¥¥*

NAGASAKI DEJIMA WHARF (長崎出島ワーフ)

At this former pier you can choose between cafés, restaurants and bars, serving Westernised, Chinese and Japanese cuisine and all with waterside views. *Daily | 1-1-109 Dejimamachi | 出島町1-1-109 | dejimawharf.com/en | Dejima tram station*

SHOPPING

NAKANOYA HATATEN (中の家旗店)

Here you can get the half-length slit curtains *(noren)* which often cover the entrances to Japanese shops and restaurants. Another nice souvenir are towels printed with traditional motifs *(tenugui)*, which, when framed, make great wall decorations. *Mon–Sat 9am–7pm, Sun 10.30am–6pm | 1-11 Kajiyamachi | 鍛冶屋町1-11 | Shiambashi tram station*

AROUND NAGASAKI

5 GUNKANJIMA (軍艦島) ★
20km from Nagasaki / 3½ hrs by ferry

Even James Bond has visited this island!! Well, almost. For the film *Skyfall* (2012), filmmakers reconstructed "Battleship Island" elsewhere. Coal was mined here from the end of the 19th century. In its heyday, the island was home to more than 5,000 people, and at only 480m long and 150m wide, it therefore had the highest population density in the world! Since the mine was shut down in 1974, everything has been crumbling away – which gives the place a unique atmosphere. Various operators offer tours, e.g. *Gunkanjima Concierge (two tours a day | from 4,000 yen |1-60 Tokiwa-cho, Tokiwa Terminal Building No. 102 | gunkanjima-concierge.com/en | ⏱ 3–4 hrs). ⧉ B9*

KAGOSHIMA

(⧉ B10) **Kagoshima (pop. 597,000) is among the most beautiful cities in Japan, mainly because of its location in the bay of the same name, directly opposite the volcanic island of Sakurajima and backing onto the majestic Kirishima range of volcanoes.**

Throughout the country, the city is known for its delicious *kurobuta* pork and for sweet potatoes, which are also distilled to produce *imojochu* liqueur.

SIGHTSEEING

SENGAN-EN GARDEN (仙巌園) ⚑
You simply must see this extensive garden with ponds, streams, bamboo trees and conifers – ideally in comfortable shoes. It is laid out so that the silhouette of the Sakurajima volcano in the backdrop can be seen in all its glory. Here, you will also find foundations, buildings and furnaces from the beginning of industrialisation during the Meiji period. It's now a UNESCO World Heritage Sites. *Daily 8.30am–5.30pm | admission 1,000 yen | 9700-1 Yoshinocho |* 吉野町 9700-1 | *senganen.jp/en | Sengan-en bus station | ⊙ 2 hrs*

AROUND KAGOSHIMA

6 SAKURAJIMA (桜島) ★
20km from Kagoshima / 15 mins by ferry
Several times each day, thick grey clouds of ash rise to the sky and rock is ejected from three 1,000m-high craters: Sakurajima is one of Japan's most active volcanoes. Therefore, access within a 2km radius is prohibited. Despite the risk, the island is home to 5,000 people. It is best to visit the sights in one of the tourist coaches. *Ferry from Kagoshima port every 15–30 mins around the clock |*

single tickets 160 yen, Sakurajima day tickets 500 yen, day tickets incl. Kagoshima 1,000 yen | 🗺 B10

7 KIRISHIMA-KINKOWAN NATIONAL PARK (霧島国立公園)
60km from Kagoshima / 1¼ hrs by car
Mythology, hiking and hot springs – welcome to one of Japan's most beautiful national parks. The mountain range comprises several volcanoes. It's an arduous ascent *(4–6 hrs)* across sharp-edged volcanic rock to the peak of 1,574-m-high *Mount Takachiho-no-mine*, but you'll be rewarded with great 360-degree views of the fascinating moon-like landscape of this range, including to the south of Kyushu. Please note that even at the *Takachiho-gawara visitor centre* there is no mobile phone

INSIDER TIP
Good for your skin

signal. Afterwards, relax in the mud oasis of the *Sakura-Sakura ryokan (2324-7 Kirishima Taguchi, Kirishima-shi | sakura-sakura.jp/en)* and breathe in the peaceful atmosphere at the wonderful *Kirishima-jingu Shrine* with its ancient trees. ▥ *B9*

⑧ CHIRAN (知覧) 🚩
40km from Kagoshima / 1 hr and 20 mins by bus

Take a tour through this interesting small town. Explore the beautiful gardens of the *samurai houses (daily 9am–5pm | admission 500 yen | 13731-1 Chiranchokori, Minamikyushu-shi, Kagoshima-ken | chiran-bukeyashiki.com/publics/index/10 | Bukeyashiki-Iriguchi buis station | ⏱ 1½–2 hrs)*; buy some famous Chiran tea, a premium Sencha tea that is tender and aromatic, and visit the *Chiran Tokko-Heiwa-Kaikan Museum (daily 9am–5pm | admission 500 yen, English audio guide 200 yen | 17881 Kori, Chiran-cho, Minamikyushu-shi, Kagoshima-ken | chiran-tokkou.jp/english/index.html | Tokko-Kannon-Iriguchi bus station | ⏱ 1½ hrs)*, which exhibits touching farewell letters written by kamikaze pilots to their families. They took off from Chiran Airfield on their suicide missions. ▥ *B10*

⑨ IBUSUKI (指宿温泉)
48km from Kagoshima / 50 mins by train

Bathing in sand? Try it at the southern tip of the Satsuma Peninsula. In the *Saraku Sand Bath (daily 8.30am–8.30pm | admission 1,080 yen | 5-25-18 Yunohama, Ibusuki-shi, Kagoshima-ken | sa-raku.sakura.ne.jp/en | 20 mins on foot from Ibusuki railway station)*

It looks awesome, but it's best to keep a safe distance from the active Sakurajima volcano

Monkeys queue to be groomed on Yakushima Beach

you lie right on the beach, protected by awnings. While wearing a *yukata*, you are covered in sand from your toes to the neck. The volcanic heat warms the sand to 50–55°C, thereby enhancing circulation. ⌘ B10

YAKUSHIMA

(⌘ B10) **Subtropical beaches combined with alpine flora and fauna have given ★ Yakushima (pop. 13,000) the nickname "Alps of the sea".**

The island has 2,000-m-high mountains and the oldest cedar forests in Japan. People say that it rains here for "35 days each month". The forest in the western part, habitat of monkeys and deer, is a UNESCO World Heritage Site. Why not hire a car to drive round the island, allowing you to stop

INSIDER TIP
Take a picture

for a photo whenever you want. Between May and July, huge turtles lay their eggs on sandy *Inakahama Beach* in the island's north-west, with the hatchlings appearing between July and October. Please keep your distance and don't use a flash.

SPORT & ACTIVITIES

A fairy wood? An enchanted place? The lush green *Shiratani Unsuikyo nature reserve (admission 500 yen)* is great for hiking and has cedars that are thousands of years old. The well-known Ghibli anime *Princess Mononoke* was allegedly modelled on this valley. Follow the clear signposts and accessible paths through the reserve. Alternatively, you can admire the big evergreen trees in the *Yakusugi Land nature reserve (admission 500 yen)*, where easy trails of different lengths take you through moss-green forest. It takes twelve hours to hike to the Jomonsugi cedar, which could be as old as 7,000 years and is best reached with the help of a local guide.

SHOPPING

Mitake Shochu is one of Japan's best sweet potato spirits, distilled on Yakushima and, in winter, drunk diluted in hot water. *The Arts & Crafts Studio Shinpachino* has been selling the master potter's hand-made, rustic wares since 1972 *(daily 8.30am–6.30pm | for directions visit yakushimayaki.com).*

INSIDER TIP
Unique pottery

OKINAWA

(□ 0) **Their subtropical climate makes the approx. 150 islands in Japan's most southerly prefecture a dream destination for beach and watersports lovers.**

Okinawa (pop. 1.4 million) is seen as the "island of longevity" due to a high percentage of elderly people here, who benefit from a healthy diet, exercise and social contact. Nowhere else are the Japanese more relaxed

and approachable. As one example, officials in Okinawa wear Hawaii shirts instead of suits.

For centuries, Okinawa was an independent kingdom with its own language and close cultural ties with China. In the early 17th century, it came under the control of the southern Japanese Satsuma clan, and in 1879 it was annexed by Japan. After the Battle of Okinawa in 1945, it remained under US administration until 1972. Today, tens of thousands of US soldiers remain stationed here. The situation is not entirely free from tension, with the occasional incident between military personnel and local people.

The best starting point for your Okinawa trip is *Naha* (pop. 323,000), capital of the biggest island with the largest population. Almost completely destroyed during World War II, today Naha is a lively cosmopolitan city with holiday vibes similar to Hawaii, which is on the same latitude.

SIGHTSEEING

SHURI-JO (首里城)

The 14th-century castle – a UNESCO World Heritage Site and Okinawa landmark – was one of the most beautiful and extraordinary castles in the country, glittering in a lacquer red, with colourful Chinese decoration – until 31 October 2019 when a fire destroyed six of the main buildings. The reconstruction work may take many years *(updates at oki-prk.jp/shurijo/en)*. Currently, only a small part can be visited. *Dec–March daily*

8am–6.30pm, April–June, Oct/Nov 8.30am–7pm, July–Sept 8.30am–8pm | admission 820 yen | 1-2 Kinjo-cho, Shuri, Naha-shi, Okinawa-ken | 沖縄県那覇市首里金城町1-2 | Shurijo-koen-iriguchi bus station

WHALE WATCHING ★ 🎦

From late December to early April whales congregate around Okinawa – a great opportunity to see these giants of the oceans at close range. Take a speedboat (50 mins) or the ferry (120 mins) from Naha to Zamami-jima Island, which belongs to the Kerama-shoto group of islands. Tours depart from there every day at 10.30am and 1pm (2½hrs, tickets 5,400 yen, children (6–11) 2,700 yen, children up to 5 free | book at whale@vill.zamami. okinawa.jp). Zamami's glorious sandy beaches are great for relaxing, such as Furuzamami in the east and Ama in the south.

OKINAWA CHURAUMI AQUARIUM (美ら海水族館) 🎦 ⛱

With 77 tanks, Japan's best aquarium is also one of the world's largest. The Kuroshio tank, which simulates the warm current that is essential to Japan's climate, holds 7,500m³ of water and contains a huge whale shark and Manta rays. The deep sea tanks are also exciting, with fish that radiate light and fierce-looking crabs. Outside are outdoor tanks with turtles, dugongs and dolphins. Oct–Feb daily 8.30am–6.30pm, March–Sept 8.30am–8pm, closed 1st Wed/Thu in Dec | admission 1,850 yen, students (from 16) 1,230 yen, students (up to 15) 610 yen, children under 6 admission free; 🎦 discounted admission from 4pm | 424 Ishikawa, Motobu-cho, Kunigami-gun | 国頭郡本部町石川424 | Yanbaru Express Bus ab Naha | ⏱ 3–4 hrs

ZUISEN SHUZO DISTILLERY (瑞泉酒造)

Awamori, the local Okinawa spirit, is made from a special kind of rice and koji mushroom spores. If you are invited to try awamori, be warned that it contains up to 60 per cent alcohol! The distillery from 1887 is only a 10-minute walk from Shuri Castle above Naha. Following a brief tour, the friendly assistant explains interesting details during a tasting session. Daily 9am–5pm | 🎫 tour & tasting free, no obligation to buy | 1-35 Shuri Sakiyamacho, Naha-shi | 那覇市首里崎山町1-35 | zuisen.co.jp/e/index. html | ⏱ 30 mins

OKINAWA PREFECTURAL PEACE MEMORIAL MUSEUM (沖縄県立平和祈念資料館)

Okinawa is the only part of Japan ever to have been invaded. Brutal battles took place here in 1945 during the last three months of the Pacific War: the "typhoon of steel" left more than 200,000 Okinawans dead, half of them civilians. The museum by the sea is dedicated to this gruesome chapter of history. The names of all victims irrespective of nationality are engraved on heavy black stones. Daily 9am–5pm, closed 29 Dec–3 Jan | admission 300 yen | 614-1 Mabuni, Itoman-shi | 糸満

市字摩文仁*614-1* | *peace-museum.pref.okinawa.jp/english* |*Heiwa-kinendo-iriguchi bus station*

KOKUSAI DORI (国際通り)

Naha's 1.6-km long "international street", as its name translates, has everything from tourist kitsch, trendy clothes and jewellery to arts and crafts, such as ceramic Shisa lions, and local specialities, such as sweet potato cakes. If you are really hungry, there are lots of restaurants to choose from, including those with evening live music.

BEACHES

Okinawa is famous for its beaches. The bathing season lasts from April to October. Beware the extremely strong sun, especially in July/August. Wear *rash vests* (long-sleeved sun protection tops) and bathing shoes; watch out for currents and jellyfish (if stung, apply vinegar).

A 15-minute drive takes you from Naha Airport to 700-m-long *Toyosaki Chura Sun Beach (5-1 Toyosaki, Tomigusuku)*, where white sand, turquoise sea, a nice café and barbecue areas await. The centre of Okinawa has popular, fine sandy *Manza Beach (Seragaki, Onna-son)* and *Nirai Beach (600 Aza-Gima, Yomitan-son)*, with plenty of water-sports opportunities. *Emerald Beach (424 Ishikawa, Motobucho)* in the north is known for its premium water quality and safety. It is next to the Okinawa-Churaumi Aquarium. And another dream location: the white sands of *Okuma Beach (913 Okuma)* are entirely natural and surrounded by wild Yanbaru woods.

An unforgettable moment: an ocean giant dives into the deep

DISCOVERY TOURS

Do you want to get under the skin of the country? Then our discovery tours provide the perfect guide – they include advice on which sights to visit, tips on where to stop for that perfect holiday snap, a choice of the best places to eat and drink, and suggestions for fun activities.

❶ ART & ARCHITECTURE BY THE SEA

➤ Discover art installations and museums
➤ Admire the sky and relax in a bathhouse
➤ Enjoy meditative and modern art

📍 Okayama railway station

🔄 132km

🏁 Okayama railway station

⛴ 2 days, ferry crossing approx. 2 hrs, cycling approx. 1 hr

ℹ️ Book tickets for the ❹ Chichu Art Museum for a specific time online in advance at e-tix.jp/chichu/en. Definitely book your room in the ❺ Benesse House early!

Perforated sculpture on Naoshima Beach

PUMPKIN MEETS LADYBIRD

Start at ❶ Okayama railway station ➤ p. 104 and take the local train (JR Uno line) to Uno railway station and the ferry terminal. The crossing to ★ Naoshima Island takes approx. 20 minutes. From a distance you can already spot a giant sculpture on the shore, looking something like a cross between a pumpkin and a ladybird – the trademark of artist Yayoi Kusama. The ❷ Miyanoura ferry terminal, whose white roof seems to float on thin columns, was designed by award-winning SANAA architects.

ALONG THE BEACH TO THE MUSEUM

Once or twice an hour, free shuttle buses take you from the harbour to the highlights of the small island, which measures just 14km². Exit at Nokyo-mae bus stop in ❸ Honmura harbour where you can visit several buildings *(Tue–Sun 10am–4.30pm | admission 1,030 yen for six buildings, 410 yen for each one)* which remained unoccupied until they were recently redecorated by artists in a playful and creative manner. For lunch, the apron cafe *(Tue–Sun 11am–4pm | ¥)* serves lovingly presented dishes. *Then take the bus to Tsutsujiso bus stop.* From here, walk along the beaches to the Chichu Art Museum.

DAY 1

❶ **Okayama railway station**

39km | 84 mins

❷ **Miyanoura**

2km | 2 mins

❸ **Honmura harbour**

4km | 45 mins

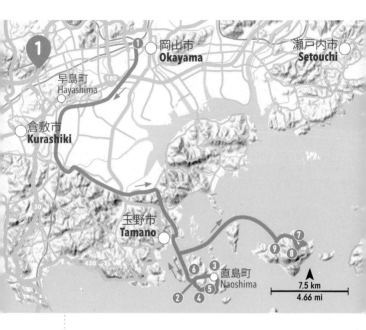

COLD CONCRETE & LOTS OF NATURAL LIGHT

Tadao Ando has designed several buildings on Naoshima, the best-known of which is the ❹ Chichu Art Museum *(March–Sept Tue–Sun 10am–6pm, Oct–Feb 10am–5pm, closed on irregular days | admission 2,060 yen | 3449-1, Naoshima-cho)*. Large parts of the building are underground and made of exposed concrete. However, the artworks are illuminated by lots of natural light. The collection is manageable, but impressive, featuring works by Claude Monet and James Turrell. Is this the real sky above the *Open Sky* artwork or merely an ingeniously lit ceiling? During the 45-minute night-time programme at sunset, you can experience the light installation again in a different atmosphere *(Fri/Sat, book in advance at yoyaku-chichu.jp/e)*.

INSIDER TIP
Evening light

FROM REFINED TO KITSCH

Treat yourself to a stay at the refined ❺ Benesse House *(Gotanji, Naoshiima-cho | benesse-artsite.jp/en/art/*

❹ Chichu Art Museum

2km   33 mins

❺ Benesse House

4km   3 mins

benessehouse-museum.html | ¥¥¥) and enjoy an exquisite dinner. Conclude the evening in Japanese style with a bath in the ⑥ I Love Yu *(Tue–Sun 1–9pm | admission 650 yen)* bathhouse in Miyanoura, designed by artist Shinro Otake in an eccentric mixture of styles.

ACROSS THE ISLAND ON AN E-BIKE

The next morning, *board the ferry to* Teshima. Hire an e-bike *(from 1,000 yen)* at the terminal, where you also get a map of all open-air art installations including distances. The best-known attraction is the 7 ⑦ Teshima Art Museum *(March–Oct Wed–Mon 10am–5pm, Nov–Feb Wed–Mon 10am–4pm, Dec–Feb Fri–Mon 10am–4pm | admission 1,540 yen | 607 Karato, Teshima | benesse-artsite.jp/en/art/teshima-artmuseum.html),* in itself an artwork and incredibly meditative. White and UFO-shaped, it has "pores" in the floor from which water rises as if it were a living organism!

LISTEN TO THE SOUNDS OF YOUR HEART!

In ⑧ Karato in the north-east of the island you can take a break in the rustic-to-trendy Shima Kitchen restaurant *(Sat–Mon 11am–4pm | ¥¥).* Then continue to a

⑥ I Love Yu

DAY 2

19km   51 mins

⑦ Teshima Art Museum

1km   10 mins

⑧ Karato

The view from Benesse House is simply stunning!

beach on the edge of Karato where you find a house named Les Archives du Cœur *(Wed–Sun 10am–5pm | admission free)*. Here you can listen to the sounds of other visitors' hearts and record your own.

YET ANOTHER MUSEUM

Don't leave the island without having visited  ❾ Teshima Yokoo House *(March–Oct Wed–Mon 10am–5pm, Nov–Feb Wed–Mon 10am–4pm, Dec–Feb Fri–Mon 10am–4pm | admission 510 yen | benesse-artsite.jp/en/art/teshima-yokoohouse.html)*. It exhibits modern paintings and exciting new takes on traditional motifs, such as a stone garden where the stones are painted red. Take the ferry back to Uno and ❶ Okayama railway station.

8 km   37 mins.

❾ Teshima Yokoo House

53 km   58 mins.

❶ Okayama railway station

❷ AMAKUSA ISLANDS TOUR

➤ Unspoilt nature: remote sandy beaches, mudflats and wild dolphins
➤ Immerse yourself in the history of "hidden Christians" and samurai
➤ Buy creative items and have a go at the potter's wheel

📍 Kumamoto

🏁 Izumi

➡ 248km

🚗 4 days (5 hrs total driving time)

ℹ ❺ Sakitsu: to visit the church, you need to book in advance at *kyoukaigun.jp/en/reserve/?cid=18*.

FROM A CAVE BATH TO A FEAST

On the Amakusa Islands you can still be a proper explorer off the beaten tourist track. In ❶ Kumamoto ➤ p. 123, *around lunch time*, hire a car which, in 45 minutes, gets you to ❷ Okoshiki Kaigan Beach near Oda railway station. At low tide, you can spot beautiful wave patterns there. This is a wonderful place for hiking on the mudflats and taking pictures! A few minutes down the road, on Oyano-jima Island, is your destination for

DAY 1

❶ Kumamoto

27km   45 mins

❷ Okoshiki Kaigan

22km	30 minz

❸ Yurakutei

the night: the ❸ **Yurakutei** ryokan hotel *(Yurakutei, 5190-2, Oyanomachikami Yumigahama, Kamiamakusa | yurakutei.jp | ¥¥)* in **Yumigahama Onsen**. Skip the afternoon snack and take some time before dinner to view your hotel, which has been managed by the same family for three generations; don't miss the unique "cave bath" which the owners carved out of the rock themselves. Put on your *yukata* cotton kimono for dinner in your generous room – a true feast, with each course being more delicious than the previous one!

4km	3 mins

DAY 2

A FEARLESS REBEL

After breakfast, visit the ❹ **Amakusa Shiro Museum** *(daily 9am–5pm, closed 2nd Tue in Jan/June | admission 600 yen | 977-1 Oyanomachinaka, Kamiamakusa-shi)*. Here you'll learn why, in the 17th century, a 16-year-old led a Christian rebellion against the military rulers – with dramatic results. 300 original items demonstrate the fate of Japanese Christians who were threatened with the death penalty.

❹ Amakusa Shiro Museum

35km	40 mins

HAVE A GO AT THE POTTER'S WHEEL

Your next destination is the potters' city of ⑤ Amakusa on the third island: Shimoshima. Most potteries allow you to have a go yourself *(amakusatoujiki.com)*. Maruoyaki-Kamamoto *(daily 10am–6.30pm | 3-10 Kitaharamachi | ¥)* in the city centre has a wide selection of light and dark bits of clay: not too fine and not to coarse either. If you are early, have lunch in the Yamanokuchi-Shokudo *(1755-3 Hondo-machi)* between 11.30am and 2pm – on matching ceramic plates from the pottery and gallery next door.

CULTURE & RELAXATION

Those who are interested in history can learn more about Japan's "hidden Christians" (who were portrayed by director Martin Scorsese in his 2016 film *Silence*) in the excellent Amakusa Christian Museum *(daily 8.30am–6pm | admission 300 yen | 19-52 Funeno-o-machi)*. In winter, end your day in the 🐋 Perla-no-Yubune open-air bath *(daily 5–8am and 11am–11pm | adults 600 yen, children 300 Yen | 996 Hirose, Hondo-machi)* with ocean views, and in summer visit Hondo Beach. The Alegria Gardens Amakusa *(hotel-alegria.jp/en/category/pelra)* is located between the open-air bath and the beach.

WATCH DOLPHINS & ENJOY CASTLE VIEWS

The next day, continue to the north coast. From ⑥ Itsuwamachi, board a boat for 🐋 dolphin watching *(departure times 10am, 11.30am, 1pm, 2.30pm, 4pm, duration 1 hr | adults 2,500 yen, children (6–12) 1,500 yen, (2–5) 500 yen | bookings on 0969 26 45 00, daily 8am–8pm)*. These waters are home to approx. 200 wild and curious dolphins. *Then follow the coastal road to the turning to* Tomioka Castle *(Thu–Tue 9am–4.45pm | admission free | 2245-15 Tomioka)* from where you have great 360-degree views. If you are hungry, ⑦ Tomioka has several restaurants. *After that, follow the west coast southbound towards Sakitsu, initially on the main road.* Up to 80 per cent of Japan's "white gold" (porcelain clay) comes from Amakusa, which is why many porcelain manufacturers have settled here.

Boat tours are a great way to see wild dolphins

Browse the beautiful crockery at ⑧ Takahamayaki Juhogama *(daily 8.30am–5pm | 598 Takahama-minami).*

⑧ Takahamayaki Juhogama

10km 7 mins

FISHING VILLAGE & WATERBED

Turn off onto the Sunset Line. It leads round pretty bays and beaches along the waterfront to the fishing village of ⑨ Sakitsu. The village and its Christian tradition was declared a UNESCO World Heritage Site in 2018. The Catholic Sakitsu Church *(Mon–Sat 9am–5pm, Sun 9.30am–5pm | admission free | 539 Kawaura-machi)* from 1569 was the centre of Christianity on Amakusa. Take some time for a walk through this charming quarter. You can stay overnight in the Kawaura Kaijo Cottages *(amuri-onsen.jp)* which have their own barbecue area and are built out over the water.

⑨ Sakitsu

12km 33 mins

TURTLES ON A REMOTE BEACH

The next morning drive to the city of Ushibuka-machi. To the west is idyllic ⑩ Mogushi Beach, where black volcanic rock on the shore contrasts with the fine light

DAY 4
⑩ Mogushi Beach

31km 19 mins

⑪ **Kuranomoto**
40km 50 mins
⑫ **Izumi**

sand. In May and June, turtles come here to lay their eggs.

TEA CEREMONY IN YOUR KIMONO

Enjoy great panoramic views during the *ferry crossing from Ushibuka to* ⑪ Kuranomoto *on* Nagashima Island. Then another hour by car gets you to the *samurai city of* ⑫ Izumi. Before exploring it, try the hand-made *soba* buckwheat noodles at Gushoan *(daily from 11am until they run out of noodles | 10-33 Fumoto-cho, Izumi-shi, Kagoshima-ken | ¥)* in a traditional house with a garden. Of the 150 houses from the Edo period, several samurai residences are open to the public, such as Takemiya and Takezoetei, where you are welcome to try on samurai armour. If booked in advance *(7,000 yen for women, from 3,000 yen for men | p.kagoshima. izumi.city@c_kanko)*, you can choose a kimono or *yukata*, put it on, stroll through the neighbourhood and wear it for a tea ceremony. Best of all: women may keep their kimono, including the belt!

INSIDER TIP
Keep your kimono

Five bridges connect the Amakusa Islands with the mainland

❸ HIKING ON THE MICHINOKU COASTAL TRAIL

➤ Take a boat along the Sanriku coast
➤ Watch bald eagles on cliffs and pine-covered rocks
➤ Birch forest, bathing stops and magnificent views

📍 Fudai railway station

🚩 Park Hotel Yodogahama

→ 90km (27km on foot, 63km by boat and train)

🥾 3 days (7 hrs total walking time)

ℹ️ Before you set off, you absolutely should buy English maps online *(tohoku.env.go.jp/mct/english)*, and also take a torch. Mobile phone coverage is patchy!
If you feel an earthquake tremor, seek higher ground immediately: there's a risk of tsunamis!
Fix a small bell to your backpack to warn off the bears or play music. While bear attacks are rare, they tend to increase in the autumn.
Certain sections of the coastal path are unpassable at high tide, but diversions are signposted.

TSUNAMI SEA WALL

Start at ❶ Fudai railway station on the Kita-Rias line of the Sanriku-Tetsudo railway. *Turn to the north-west and walk underneath the tracks to the* ❷ Fudai-Suimon weir. In 2011, this massive weir saved the inhabitants from the tsunami – thanks to a visionary mayor who had previously insisted on its construction costing 3.5 billion yen (28 million euros) against strong local opposition. A blue line shows the level of the flood waters: 23.5m above sea level.

JUMP INTO THE WAVES

On ❸ Fudai Beach is a layby with the Kiraumi food stall *(Wed–Mon 10am–5pm)* and showers for a bathing

DAY 1

❶ Fudai railway station
2km   35 mins

❷ Fudai-Suimon

0.5km   8 mins

❸ Fudai Beach
1.3km   16 mins

❹ Otanabe-bochotei embankment
1.5km · 29 mins

❺ Nedari Nature Trail
2.6km · 35 mins

❻ Kurosaki viewpoint
0.6km · 11 mins

❼ Kokumin Shukusha Kurosakiso
0.2km · 7 mins

DAY 2

❽ Anmoura viewpoint and waterfall
4.8km · 1 hr 2 mins

❾ Kitayamazaki viewpoint
9.1km · 2 hrs 13 mins

❿ Tanohata-mura

DAY 3
3.7km · 58 mins

⓫ Shimanokoshi
7km · 50 mins

⓬ Kitayamzaki cliffs

stop in summer are nearby. *Follow the hiking trail along the coast* past the ❹ Otanabe-bochotei embankment. Look up: can you see the red gate leading to the small shrine? In 2011, it served as a refuge from the big wave.

STEEP CLIFFS & GREAT VIEWS

Soon you get to the ❺ Nedari Nature Trail, one of the most beautiful sections with folded rock formations and steep pine-covered cliffs. From a cove, *mossy steps and tracks lead uphill to the* ❻ Kurosaki viewpoint with incredible coastline views! Beware of the bears that are sometimes seen in this place. 600m further on, the ❼ Kokumin Shukusha Kurosakiso *(84-4 Shimomura, Dainichiwari, Fudai-mura | tel. 0194 35 26 11 | ¥)* offers Japanese rooms and delicious local specialities.

... AND MORE PANORAMIC VIEWS

The next morning, after a photo stop at the ❽ Anmoura viewpoint and waterfall, continue high above the coast to the ❾ Kitayamazaki viewpoint, 200m above sea level, a highlight in the Sanriku-Fukko National Park ➤ p. 51. Afterwards, it's the perfect time for a lunch stop at the Kitayamazaki Resthouse *(May–Nov daily 8.30am–4pm | ¥)*. Why not try *ramen* noodles with seafood?

FROM BIRCH FORESTS TO THE UNDERWORLD

The journey continues through birch forests, in parts along cliffs and through unlit tunnels, carved out of the rock by hand. Your destination is the village of ❿ Tanohata-mura, where you can see the Ragaso Hotel *(60-1 Raga, Tanohata-mura, Shimohei-gun | ¥¥)* by the water. The spacious tatami rooms offer great ocean views. The food is plentiful and delicious, including lots of fresh seafood.

BOAT TOUR TO THE CLIFFS

After a generous Japanese breakfast, *follow the hiking trail* to the harbour of ⓫ Shimanokoshi. From here, sightseeing boats carry you to the ⓬ Kitayamazaki cliffs, 7km away, at least four times a day between late

April and early November *(tickets 1,460 yen)*. You'll see bald eagles overhead, and you can feel the power of the waves below the boat.

IDYLLIC COASTAL TRACKS TO DREAM BEACHES

From the harbour it is only a short distance to Shimanokoshi railway station. The train takes 44 minutes to reach ⑬ Miyako, from where regular buses take you to the ⑭ Kankyosho Jodogahama Visitor Center *(daily 8am–6pm | 32-59 Hitachihama-cho | jodogahama-vc.jp)* which has a great exhibition about the region. Then take tracks and hiking trails along a picturesque stretch of coastline – past craggy rocks and pine trees. In summer you can bathe here and go on boat tours. Your accommodation is close by: in the ⑮ Park Hotel Jodogahama *(32-32-4 Hitachihamacho | jodo-ph.jp/eng | ¥¥¥)* above the beach you can enjoy a delicious buffet to celebrate the end of your hike. If you like experimenting, try the local kegani speciality, a hairy crab.

50km 1 hr 34 mins

⑬ Miyako
5.7km 6 mins

⑭ Kankyosho Jodogahama Visitor Center
0.9km 18 mins

⑮ Park Hotel Jodogahama

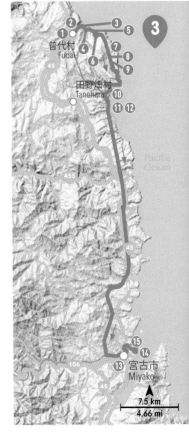

普代村
Fudai

田野畑村
Tanohara

Pacific Ocean

宮古市
Miyako

7.5 km
4.66 mi

GOOD TO KNOW

HOLIDAY BASICS

ARRIVAL

Flights from the UK take 12 to 13 hours plus another six hours or so if you have connecting flights in-between. In Japan it is required by law that you must carry your passport with you. In Tokyo, Haneda Airport is practical due to its proximity to the city.

 Adapter type A

Japan operates a 100-volt AC mains system (UK uses 220 volt). Although most chargers for your camera, laptop and smartphone work with that voltage, you will need an adapter for sockets with two non-polarised pins (SE -> A) which are available at reasonable prices in Japan.

From here, a taxi will take you to the city centre for approx. 60 euros, while trains cost about six euros. A taxi from the city's other airport, Narita, costs almost 200 euros! Alternatives from Narita include airport buses (e.g. Keisei from seven euros) or trains (from seven euros). The bus takes about one hour to Tokyo railway station and approx. 90 minutes to the larger hotels *(limousinebus.co.jp/en)*.

IMMIGRATION
All visitors must have a passport that is valid for the duration of the visit. British and US citizens can enter Japan as a visitor for up to 90 days without a visa (you will receive a 90-day visa on arrival; citizens of the UK can extend their visit for a further three months on application). Please note that you may need to provide evidence of a return/onward ticket.

箱根湯本

1002

箱根
あじさい
電車
HAKONE TOZAN RAILWAY

Cheap, practical and on time: trains are Japan's best means of transport

+8 or +9 hour time difference

Japan is 9 hours ahead of Greenwhich Mean Time (GMT) and 8 hours ahead during British Summer Time.

CLIMATE & WHEN TO GO

Japan has big temperature differences, from an average 9.5°C on Hokkaido in the north to 16.5°C in Tokyo and 23.5°C on Okinawa in the south. Best travel times are spring and autumn, because in summer the weather can be overcast and grey as this is the rainy season. July, August and September are frequently humid with temperatures above 35°C. Japanese winters are sunny, dry and mild on the east coast, but cold and snowy by the Sea of Japan. Okinawa is good for bathing between May and October, while the bathing season in the rest of the country is from July to August. It is best to avoid visiting Japan during "Golden Week" from late April to early May as well as around the *obon* celebrations in mid-August and over New Year, as the country is busy, prices are high, public transport is overcrowded and everything is fully booked.

INSIDER TIP
Avoid peak times

CUSTOMS

You are advised not to travel to Japan with sausage and meat products because you will get into trouble at the airport. Importing certain medication is also prohibited. However, you may bring up to three bottles of alcoholic beverages (at 760ml) and up to 200 cigarettes into the country. Export of (valuable) cultural artefacts and antiques requires formal approval by the relevant authority.

GETTING AROUND

AT THE AIRPORT
Make sure that you take out cash at the airport because going to banks is both complicated and time-consuming. Also redeem your Japan Rail Pass voucher at the airport. Airports also offer SIM card, mobile phone and Wi-Fi router hire.

HIRE CARS
Vehicles drive on the left-hand side of the road, as in the UK. Most foreign visitors (including UK and US citizens) require an International Driving Permit (IDP) to drive in Japan. The IDP must be obtained in your home country before travelling. The speed limit in towns and villages is between 30 and 50kmh, outside towns 60–80kmh and on motorways 80–100kmh. The legal alcohol limit is 0.3 per ml. Using mobile phones at the wheel is strictly prohibited. Hiring a car with Sat Nav (book in advance!) costs 40–60 euros per day including insurance.

TAXIS
In Tokyo, the rate per kilometre is 3.30 euros (410 yen), and then 1.90 euros per 237m. A 20% surcharge applies between 10pm and 5am. City centres have many taxis which you flag down – ideally in the direction in which you want to go. If a taxi displays a red sign at the windscreen, it is available. Uber doesn't operate in Japan – try the JapanTaxi app instead.

DOMESTIC FLIGHTS
The big airlines JAL and ANA offer tourists many promotions and discounts – although most of them need to be booked before you come to Japan. Big budget airlines include Jetstar Japan, Peach Aviation and Skymark Airlines. Flights can be up to 20% cheaper in the early morning and late evening.

FERRIES
From Tokyo you can take the overnight ferry to the Izu Islands and wake up to unspoilt nature. Discount tickets can be up to 30% cheaper. In the Seto Inland Sea, the ferry is often also the best means of transport.

TRAINS
Trains are the ideal means of transport in Japan – cheap, practical and punctual. The rail network covers almost every corner of the country. The more often you need to change operators, e.g.

INSIDER TIP
Stay with on operator

in Tokyo from Japan Rail (JR) to Metro or Toei Metro, the more expensive it gets. If you plan to visit several cities, get a *Japan Rail Pass (japanrailpass. net/de/index.html)* for one, two or three weeks before coming to Japan, because a return journey from Tokyo to Kyoto already costs roughly the same as a Japan Rail Pass for a whole week. A cheaper option are the *Seishun Juhachi Kippu tickets (jreast. co.jp/e/pass/seishun18.html)*, but these are only available in Japan and only apply to slower trains and certain time periods.

FESTIVALS & EVENTS
ALL YEAR ROUND

JANUARY
O-shogatsu (countrywide): New Year's festival at shrines and temples

FEBRUARY
Snow Festival (Sapporo), p. 45

FEBRUARY/MARCH
Setsubun (countrywide): spring festival

MAY
Sanja Matsuri (Tokyo): traditional festival with portable shrines (photo)

JUNE
Itoman Hare (Itoman, Okinawa): dragon boat festival

JULY
Sumidagawa Hanabitaikai (Tokyo): fireworks
Gion Matsuri (Kyoto): p. 93
Hakata Gion Yamakasa (Fukuoka): p.122
Fuji Rock Festival (Naeba, Niigata): *fujirock-eng.com*

AUGUST
Nebuta Matsuri (Aomori): traditional festival, p. 49
Sendai Tanabata Matsuri (Sendai): traditional festival, p. 54
Summer fireworks (Matsue): p.110
Summer Sonic (Maihama, Chiba): music festival, summersonic.com
Earth Celebration (Sadogashima): music festival, earthcelebration.jp/en

SEPTEMBER
Jozenji Street Jazz Festival (Sendai): p. 54

OCTOBER
Naha Otsunahiki (Naha, Okinawa): tug-of-war festival

NOVEMBER
Karatsu Kunchi (Karatsu, Saga): shrine festival

DECEMBER
Chichibu Yomatsuri (Chichibu, Saitama): night-time festival

BICYCLE

Bicycles are a cheap and practical option for exploring Japan. There are countless hire companies and several cities run networks with pick-up stations.

EMERGENCIES

CONSULATES & EMBASSIES
BRITISH EMBASSY TOKYO
Ichiban-cho, Chiyoda-ku | tel. 03 52 11 11 00 | www.gov.uk.government/ world/organisations/british-embassy-tokyo

BRITISH CONSULATE GENERAL OSAKA
Bakuro-machi, Chuo-ku | tel. 06 61 20 56 00 | www.gov.uk/government/ world/organisations/british-consulate-general-osaka

U.S. EMBASSY TOKYO
Aka-saka, Minato-ku | tel. 03 32 24 50 00 | www.jp.usembassy.gov

EMERGENCY PHONE NUMBERS
Police: *1 10*
English-speaking helpline *(Mon–Fri except for public holidays 8.30am–5.15pm): tel. 03 35 01 01 10*
Ambulance, fire brigade: *119*
Tokyo English Life Line (TELL) for psychological support *(daily 9am–5pm): tel. 03 32 01 33 31*

HEALTH

The Japanese healthcare system is superb, but there are considerable language barriers. The *Himawari Medical Information Service (tel. 03 52 85 81 81 | daily 9am–8pm)* hotline provides information about surgeries, clinics and pharmacies in English. Big hospitals such as Tokyo's St. Luke's International Hospital at Tsukiji railway station and the Japan Red Cross Medical Center at Hiroo railway station have English-speaking staff.

ESSENTIALS

ACCOMMODATION

You can choose between business hotels offering a bed, European-style breakfast and sometimes tiny, but practical rooms, and Japanese hotels *(ryokan)* with a thin futon mattress on rice straw mats, generally two (filling) meals in Japanese style and fixed meal times. Treat yourself to the (sometimes quite expensive) Japanese version, at least for one night. You can pay less in *minshuku*, family-run Japanese accommodation. Single travellers may find it difficult to get a *ryokan* for one person. In Japan, prices are calculated per person, not per room.

ANIMALS

Cockroaches are off-putting but harmless, and special sprays work best to get rid of them. Mosquitos are a common nuisance in summer, but equally harmless. If you intend to stay in rural areas for long periods of time, you may want to consider getting vaccinated against Japanese encephalitis, a mosquito-transmitted viral infection of the brain. Local spiders are non-venomous. There are potentially deadly snakes in Japan, but bites are extremely rare. The northern part of the main island of Honshu and Hokkaido are bear habitats, and these animals may kill you if spooked. Avoid the time around dawn and dusk, observe the warnings and fix a little bell to your backpack as a precaution.

INTERNET & WIFI

Free Wi-Fi is increasingly available in Japan, especially in Tokyo. However, traditional *ryokan* hostels often only offer internet access in the lobby or via the wired internet connection in your room.

MONEY

Japan is a country of cash, especially in the countryside! Take out cash at the airport on arrival and then top up at cash machines where you can. Note that debit cards are not accepted, so you'll need a credit card with a PIN, and some ATMs won't accept foreign cards at all. Good alternative sources of cash are the Japan Post bank and the big convenience store chains, such as 7Eleven, FamilyMart and Lawson.

NATURAL HAZARDS

August and September are typhoon season. These storms can massively impact public transport, and the accompanying downpours can cause flooding and mudslides. In the event of severe earthquakes, seek shelter in house entrances, under door frames, under a table or on the floor by your bed. Stay calm and don't rush outside where there is an even greater risk of being hit by falling debris. Severe quakes can also trigger tsunamis. Therefore, get yourself to higher ground or onto solid tall buildings. The Japanese met office website provides up-to-date disaster warnings: *jma.go.jp*

NUDISM

Nude bathing and topless sunbathing are frowned upon in Japan. Remember that the sun is stronger than in Europe, so wear the appropriate clothing with long sleeves and legs or *rash guards* (sun protection clothes). Use sun cream with factor 50 UVA protection.

OPENING HOURS

For the big sightseeing attractions, in particular, you should be on site at least half an hour before closing time. Typical opening hours for sights are 9am–5pm and in winter often only until 4pm. Most businesses or shops open at 10 or 11am, but remain open until at least 6pm and frequently 8pm or even later.

PHOTOGRAPHS

Many temples and shrines do not permit photographs in the inner sanctum. If you want to take a picture of people, a friendly *"sumimasen"* (excuse me) and the corresponding gestures will be helpful.

POST

Postcards to Europe cost 70 yen and letters 110 yen. ATMs in post offices accept international credit cards.

PRICES

The more Japanese a product is, the cheaper it is: this applies to shopping in supermarkets. Restaurants always offer you water for free or green tea as an alternative. You are not obliged to order a drink. High-quality sushi is moderately priced. Beer and wine are more expensive than in the UK. Electronic items, which were once cheaper than in Europe and the USA, are not necessarily so these days, but you can get good, reasonably priced clothes at Uniqlo and Muji.

HOW MUCH DOES IT COST?	
Soft drink	£1
	at the vending machine
Snack	80p
	for an onigiri rice ball
Metro	80p
	for a ticket
Lunch set	£7
	for a meal
Wine	£5
	for a glass (0.2l)
Petrol	80p
	for one litre

SAFETY

Japan is a safe country to travel to, and theft and fraud are rare events. Possession and consumption of drugs are subject to severe penalties. Groping (chikan) on the train during rush-hour is a problem, and while the official figures for sex offences are low, the reality is much worse. That said, the presence of people out and about in the cities around the clock means that, as a woman, you can feel reasonably safe walking busy streets at night on your own. Nightlife and red-light districts are areas controlled by the Japanese mafia (yakuza), which is why you need to watch out for drink spiking and unregulated charges for drinks and when visiting bars.

TELEPHONE & MOBILE

To call a number in Japan, dial 0081, followed by the area code but omit the initial 0. Mobile numbers start with 070, 080 or 090. Thanks to the ever-improving Wi-Fi coverage, your smartphone should be OK in cities. However, for travel to rural areas, you are advised to hire a Wi-Fi router and/or mobile with a local SIM card at the airport.

TIPPING

Tipping is not customary in Japan, instead it might even be interpreted as insulting. A heartfelt '"thank you" will be sufficient.

TOILETS

Toilets in Japan are clean, free and numerous: every convenience store has one. In the countryside you may still encounter the odd loo where you need to crouch. Often there are neither paper towels nor a hand drier – it is best to take a small towel or wipes with you.

Vending machines at Kyoto

WEATHER IN TOKYO

	JAN	FEB	MARCH	APRIL	MAY	JUNE	JULY	AUG	SEPT	OCT	NOV	DEC
Daytime temperature												
	9°	10°	13°	18°	23°	25°	29°	31°	27°	21°	17°	12°
Night-time temperature												
	1°	2°	4°	10°	14°	18°	22°	23°	20°	14°	9°	4°
☀	6	5	5	5	6	4	4	6	4	4	5	5
🌂	4	6	9	10	10	12	10	8	11	9	6	4
≋	16	14	14	16	18	21	24	26	25	22	20	17

☀ Hours of sunshine per day   🌂 Rainy days per month   ≋ Water temperature in °C

WORDS & PHRASES
JAPANESE

SMALL TALK

Yes/no/maybe	はい/いいえ/たぶん	hai/iye/tabun
Please/thank you	どうぞ/ありがとう	douzo/arigatou
Hello/Goodbye	こんにちは/ それじゃ、またね	konnichiwa/sayounara
My name is …	… と申します	… to moushi masu
What is your name? (formal) /What is your name? (informal)	名前は何ですか/お名前を教えてください	namae ha nani desu ka?/onamae wo oshiete kudasai
I am from …	… から来ました	… kara ki mashi ta
Excuse me!	すみません	sumimasen!
Pardon? Could you repeat that please?	すみません。もう一度お願いします	Sumimasen. Mou – ichi do onegai shimasu
I (don't) like this	… は気に入りました（入りません）	… wa ki ni irimaschta (irimasen)
I would like …/Do you have …?	… を探しています	… o sagaschte imass.

SYMBOLS

EATING & DRINKING

Please reserve a table for four people for this evening.	今夜の四人分の席を予約したいのですが	Konja no joninbun no seki o jojaku schtai no dess ga.
The menu, please.	メニューをお願いします	Menjuh o onegai schimass.
Please could I have ...	... を頂いてもいいですか	... o itadaite mo ih dess ka?
salt/pepper/sugar	塩/胡椒/砂糖	schio/koschoh/satoh
bakery	パン屋	pan-ja
Market	市場	itschiba
Supermarket	スーパー	suhpah
I'd like to pay, please.	お勘定お願いします	O-kandschoh onegai schimass.
cash/credit card	現金/クレジットカード	genkin/kredschitto kahdo

MISCELLANEOUS

Where is ...?/Where are ...?	... はどこですか	... wa doko dess ka?
How much does ... cost?	... はいくらですか	... wa ikura dess ka?
What time is it?	今何時ですか	Ima nandschi dess ka?
today/tomorrow/yesterday	今日/明日/昨日	kjoh/aschta/kinoh
open/closed	開いています/閉まっています	aite-imass/schimatte-imass
right/left	右/左	migi/hidari
broken/not working	壊れています	kowarete-imass
timetable/ticket	時刻表/切符	dschikokkuhioh/kippu
internet access/WiFi	インターネット接続/無線LAN	intahnetto ssezusokku/musen-lahn
fever/pain	熱/痛み	nezzu/itami
pharmacy/chemist	薬局/ドラッグストア	jak-kjokku/draggstoa
Help!/Watch out!	助けて/気をつけて	tasskette/ki o zkette
0/1/2/3/4/5/6/7/8/9/10/100/1000	ゼロ/一/二/三/四/五/六/七/八/九/十/百/千	sero/itschi/ni/san/jonn/go/rokk/nana/hatschi/kjuh/dschuh/hjakku/ssenn

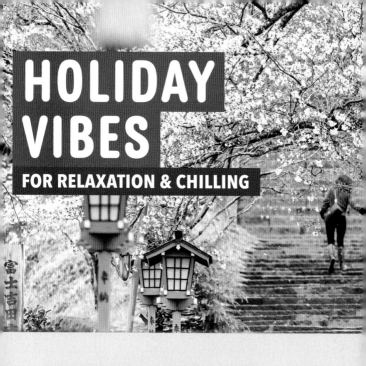

HOLIDAY VIBES

FOR RELAXATION & CHILLING

FOR BOOKWORMS & FILM BUFFS

📖 CONVENIENCE STORE WOMAN

A short novel by Sayaka Murata (2016, translated by Ginny Tapley Takemori, 2018) about the seemingly banal and uneventful life of Keiko, who rejects society's aspirations and expectations in order to work in a local convenience store.

📖 THE SILENT DEAD

First in the series of popular crime thrillers by Tetsuya Honda, featuring Lieutenant Reiko Himekawa of the Tokyo police (2006, translated by Giles Murray, 2016)

🎥 DEPARTURES

A young cellist whose orchestra is disbanded, initially applies for a job as a tour escort but then stumbles across work as a *nōkanshi* – a traditional Japanese ritual mortician. This won the Academy Award for Best Foreign Language Film in 2009 (directed by Yojiro Takita).

🎥 MY NEIGHBOR TOTORO

Animated film by Hayao Miyazaki of Studio Ghibli, which tells the story of two girls and their friendship with a spirit creature in post-war rural Japan (1988, English-language version, 2006).

PLAYLIST

0:58

❚❚ ONE OK ROCK – MIGHTY LONG FALL
High-energy alternative rock with English and Japanese lyrics and fans in Europe and the US.

▶ MASAHARU FUKUYAMA – SAIAI
A sad piano-accompanied ballad about the songwriter's lost love.

▶ KOBUKURO – TSUBOMI
One of the best-known Japanese pop songs.

▶ ANGELA AKI – TEGAMI: HAIKEI JUGO NO KIMI E
An emotional song by the singer-songwriter and pianist.

▶ SAYURI ISHIKAWA – TSUGARUKAIKYO FUYUGESHIKI
The biggest hit by one of the most successful singers of *enka* (folk songs).

The holiday soundtrack is available on **Spotify** under **MARCO POLO Japan**

Or scan this code with the Spotify app

ONLINE

GURUNAVI
The gourmet app shows you culinary delights nearby with tips by local people.

JAPAN TAXI
Similar to Uber – this English-language taxi app is good for getting about in major Japanese cities.

JAPAN TRAVEL
This app by Navitime is an all-round tool for travelling to Japan, showing maps both online and offline, where to find Wi-Fi, deposit your luggage or exchange cash.

ONLY IN JAPAN
John Daub, who speaks Japanese fluently, provides a sympathetic guide to Japan, featuring anything from the known to the eccentric in brief videos. youtube.com/user/ONLYinJAPAN WAORYU

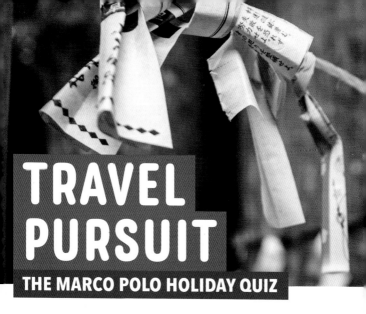

TRAVEL PURSUIT

THE MARCO POLO HOLIDAY QUIZ

Do you know what makes Japan tick? Test your knowledge of the idiosyncrasies and eccentricities of the country and its people. You'll find the answers at the foot of the page, with more detailed explanations on pp18–23.

❶ Who designed Tokyo's National Stadium for the Summer Olympics 2020?
a) Kengo Kuma
b) Zaha Hadid
c) Tadao Ando

❷ Why do visitors to temples and shrines tie white notes to the buildings?
a) They can't find a dustbin
b) They hope that the proximity to the Gods will protect them against negative energy
c) They think that it's pretty – like Christmas tree decorations in Europe

❸ How much does a Japanese man need to earn in order to be regarded as an attractive husband?
a) Money is irrelevant
b) £24,000 annually
c) £40,000 annually

❹ What is the name of the current Emperor?
a) Akihito
b) Naruhito
c) Hirohito

❺ For how long, on average, do *hikikomori*, lock themselves away in their room?
a) six months
b) three years
c) eleven years

Omikuji Charms or random fortune papers in shrines at Japan

Omikuji Charms or random fortune papers in shrines at Nikko

INDEX

CREDITS

WE WANT TO HEAR FROM YOU!

Did you have a great holiday? Is there something on your mind? Whatever it is, let us know! Whether you want to praise the guide, alert us to errors or give us a personal tip – MARCO POLO would be pleased to hear from you.
Please contact us by email:
sales@heartwoodpublishing.co.uk

We do everything we can to provide the very latest information for your trip. Nevertheless, despite all of our authors' thorough research, errors can creep in. MARCO POLO does not accept any liability for this.

PICTURE CREDITS
Cover photo: Cherry blossom (MATO/AFLO: A. Tagami). Photos: DuMont Bildarchiv: Emmler (129), Schröder/Schwarz AWL Images: M. Colombo (6/7); S. Blaschke (163); Getty Images: Bohistock (9), D. Clumpner (135), C. Court (82), Y. Hasumi (71), RichLegg (32/33); Getty Images/Corbis/Art In All Of Us: E. Lafforgue (97); Getty Images/EyeEm: L. Ono (56); Getty Images/NurPhoto: R. Atrero de Guzman (151), O. Rupeta (23); Getty Images/Yagi-Studio (110/111); huber-images: T. Draper (108), M. Rellini (158/159); R. Köhler (85); Laif: D. Gebhart de Koekkoek (115), T. Kierok (35, 74, 88), M. Kirchgessner (26/27, 30/31), F. Moleres (122), T. & B. Morandi (back cover flap, 24/25), Ch. Papsch (14/15), J. M. Park (128), J. F. Raga (100/101), J. Souteyrat (64); Laif/Arcaid: B. Simmons (58/59); Laif/hemis.fr: F. Guiziou (31, 105, 107); Laif/Le Figaro Magazine: Martin (136/137, 139); Laif/robertharding: G. Hellier (77); Look: E. Kapitza (10); Look/age fotostock (inside and outside cover flaps/1, 11, 63, 68); Look/Minden (132); mauritius images: J. F. Raga (98, 112), S. Vidler (12/13, 95), J. Warburton-Lee (2/3, 78/79); mauritius images/age fotostock: (19), L. Vallecillos (43), (50, 92); mauritius images/Alamy: Image navi QxQ images (144), T. Jones (86), S. Pavone (121), U. Switucha (55); mauritius images/Alamy/China Span: K. Su (143); mauritius images/Diversion (38/39, 46, 116/117, 130/131, 148/149); mauritius images/imagebroker: O. Maksymenko (67); mauritius images/Minden Pictures (8); mauritius images/SMART (27); mauritius images/robertharding (125); picture-alliance/AP Images: K. Muto (48/49); picture-alliance/Mint Images (20); picture-alliance/Phanie: Voisin (160); Shutterstock.com/Krikkiat (155).

2nd Edition – fully revised and updated 2023
Worldwide Distribution: Heartwood Publishing Ltd, Bath, United Kingdom
www.heartwoodpublishing.co.uk

Author: Sonja Blaschke
Editor: Karin Liebe
Picture editor: Anja Schlattere
Cartography: © MAIRDUMONT, Ostfildern (pp. 36–37, 138, 141, 147, outside jacket, pull-out map); © Shobunsha Publications, Inc. (Faltkarte Nebenkarte); © MAIRDUMONT, Ostfildern, using data from OpenStreetMap, licence CC-BY-SA 2.0 (pp.40–41, 44, 60–61, 72, 80–81, 91, 102–103, 118–119, 127)
Cover design and pull-out map cover design: bilekjaeger_Kreativagentur with Zukunftswerkstatt, Stuttgart
Page design: Langenstein Communication GmbH, Ludwigsburg

Heartwood Publishing credits:
Translated from the German by Thomas Moser and Mo Croasdale
Editors: Felicity Laughton, Kate Michell, Sophie Blacksell Jones
Prepress: Summerlane Books, Bath
Printed in India

All rights reserved. No part of this book may be reproduced, stored in a retrieval system or transmitted in any form or by any means (electronic, mechanical, photocopying, recording or otherwise) without prior written permission from the publisher.or by any means (electronic, mechanical, photocopying, recording or otherwise) without prior written permission from the publisher.

MARCO POLO AUTHOR
SONJA BLASCHKE

A passionate concert-goer and island-hopper, Sonja has lived in Japan since 2005 and loves discovering the country's unexpected side. For example, in a remote restaurant on Okinawa, she was serenaded by a waitress with a guitar and an emotional folk song. As a freelance journalist, German-born Sonja *(sonja blaschke.de)* writes about East Asia for Swiss broadsheet *Neue Züricher Zeitung* and produces films for German broadcasters such as ZDF, ARD and Arte.